A NEW CHURCH
FOR A
NEW WORLD

Other books in the Foundations of Christian Faith series

A NEW CHURCH FOR A NEW WORLD

John M. Buchanan

Foundations of Christian Faith
Published by Geneva Press in Conjunction with
the Office of Theology and Worship, Presbyterian Church (U.S.A.)

Scripture quotations from the New Revised Standard Version of the Bible are copyright © 1989 by the Division of Christian Education of the National Council of the Churches of Christ in the U.S.A. and are used by permission.

"The Creation" by James Weldon Johnson is published here by permission of Dr. Sondra Kathryn Wilson, Executor for the Estate of Grace and James Weldon Johnson.

Book design by Sharon Adams
Cover design by Night & Day Design

First edition
Published by Geneva Press
Louisville, Kentucky

This book is printed on acid-free paper that meets the American National Standards Institute Z39.48 standard. ∞

PRINTED IN THE UNITED STATES OF AMERICA

08 09 10 11 12 13 14 15 16 17 — 10 9 8 7 6 5 4 3 2 1

Library of Congress Cataloging-in-Publication Data is on file at the Library of Congress, Washington, D.C.

ISBN 978-0-664-50141-9

Contents

Series Foreword

The books in the Foundations of Christian Faith series explore central elements of Christian belief. These books are intended for persons on the edge of faith as well as for those with strong Christian commitment. The writers are women and men of vital faith and keen intellect who know what it means to be an everyday Christian.

Each of the twelve books in the series focuses on a theme central to the Christian faith. The authors hope to encourage you as you grapple with the big, important issues that accompany our faith in God. Thus, Foundations of Christian Faith includes volumes on the Trinity, what it means to be human, worship and sacraments, Jesus Christ, the Bible, the Holy Spirit, the church, life as a Christian, political and social engagement, religious pluralism, creation and new creation, and dealing with suffering.

You may read one or two of the books that deal with issues you find particularly interesting, or you may wish to read them all in order to gain a deeper understanding of your faith. You may read the books by yourself or together with others. In any event, I trust that you will find a fuller awareness of the living God who is made known in Jesus Christ through the present power of the Holy Spirit. Christian faith is not about the mastery of ideas. It is about encountering the living God. It is my confident hope that this series of books will lead you more deeply into that encounter.

Charles Wiley
Office of Theology and Worship
Presbyterian Church (U.S.A.)

Prologue

*T*he church is a people on the move, on a journey, a pilgrimage. The church is a work in progress, and every book about the church reflects and is limited by the experience of its writer and readers. This book is written by an American Presbyterian in the first decade of the twenty-first century, a critical time for the church, particularly the mainline Protestant Church in the United States of America.

The end of the second millennium and the beginning of the third constitute a birthday celebration of sorts for the church. Most of the world continues to measure time by the birth of Jesus. That event, central to Christian faith, also marks the beginning of a new phenomenon in human history: the Christian church. Three and one-half decades after his birth, small communities of Jewish followers of Jesus have come to believe that in him God has spoken and acted decisively. Some believe he was the promised Messiah, the anointed one, the Christ. They mix freely with other strands of Judaism—meeting in the Temple on the Sabbath, participating in the Temple rites and rituals—and they meet in their respective homes to talk about their experiences, their emerging faith and trust and hope in Christ. As Gentiles are attracted to and join this growing movement, communities of believers appear throughout Palestine and Asia Minor and move steadily westward into the provinces and cities of the Roman Empire. The movement has now become almost wholly Gentile, and it has taken for itself the name of the One who is its Lord, its Christ.

They are Christians, and together they are the Christian church, his church. When they are together they worship, pray, sing, break bread, and drink wine as he instructed his followers to do. And they also do something else, which is so unique that they impress their neighbors everywhere they are. They love one another. They argue and fight, but they also extend kindness and compassion. They take care of the people no one else in society cares about: unwanted infants, orphans, the sick, the elderly, the outcast. It's very impressive, this new style of life—so much so that their neighbors say of them, "See how they love another."[1]

Gradually they come to believe that they are involved in something bigger than themselves. They come to believe that God is using them.

One of the most remarkable developments in all of human history is that within three centuries, this modest movement of scattered Christian communities will have grown in numbers and influence so much that the Roman emperor, Constantine the Great, will end official persecution, and some fifty years later the emperor Theodosius will declare that Christianity is now the official religion of Rome. In earlier years the believers met in secret to avoid persecution. Outsiders, nonbelievers were not permitted to attend meetings in which bread was broken and a cup shared in memory of the Lord. One of the most dramatic transformations in all of history occurred in the fourth century as Christianity, a weak, despised, and persecuted minority cult, became the religion of the empire, a requirement of citizenship.

That transformation from outsider to insider, from persecution to official favor, constitutes the most important move in the church's history. The result is called Christendom, when Christianity becomes almost indistinguishable from the dominant culture, a status that was perpetuated in Western and Eastern Orthodox civilization until our time. Now, eighteen hundred years after Constantine and Theodosius, we are witness to the decline of Christendom, the old confluence of our religion and the dominant culture. Empty churches across Europe and the numerical decline of the mainline churches in North America signal that the old accommodation between the Christian church and Western culture is at an end. A newly energized Christian Right in the United States portrays itself as fighting for the old arrangement, traditional Christian values, and a specifically Christian culture and nation. Nevertheless, Christendom is disappearing.

One of the influential Reformed theologians of our times, Douglas John Hall, describes our new situation as the "end of Christendom"[2] but, at the same time, the promise of a hopeful new future for the Christian church.

The movement to Christendom and now away from it is an important part of our story. The end of Christendom is the context for any reflection on the church at the beginning of the twenty-first century. Gone are the days when church membership was a prerequisite for a political office or employment, when identity as a Christian was a stipulation for admission to an exclusive college, university, or private club. In this new context many are asking, explicitly or implicitly, "What's so important about the church? Why bother with the church?"

Anglican Bishop N. T. Wright defines the church not as a building nor as an institution at all, but as "the company of all those who believe in the God we see in Jesus and who are struggling to follow him." There is, that is to say, a fascinating story going on within the story of human history. It is the story of the Creator God's relationship with human beings and the long and fascinating history that ensues. With the birth, life, death, and resurrection of Jesus of Nazareth, whom Christians know as Christ, it is the story of the church. "We're called," those who believe in Jesus Christ and struggle faithfully to follow him, Bishop Wright says, "to be instruments of God's new creation, the world-put-to-right which has already been launched in Jesus and of which Jesus' followers are supposed to be not simply its beneficiaries but also agents."[3]

This small book is an attempt to tell the amazing history within history, the story of God and God's people, the church.

Chapter 1 sets the current challenges facing the church and the struggle of God's people faithfully to follow Jesus in the larger context of God and God's people and the consistent experience throughout history that God is always doing "a new thing."

Chapter 2 identifies the church as a continuation of God's creation and calling of a community, a family, within the larger human family, while chapter 3 traces early Christian history and examines the church as a part of what Christians believe when we say, in the Apostles' Creed, "I believe in the holy catholic church."

The fascinating story of the church's important role in Western civilization and its developing culture, the Roman Empire, the emergence of the papacy, and the Protestant Reformation is the focus of chapter 4.

Chapter 5 traces the stormy period of the Reformation and focuses on the Reformed/Presbyterian branch of the Reformation, moving to the Presbyterian presence in the New World and the American Revolution. In chapter 6 the evolution of the Presbyterian presence in the new United States of America expressed in social and political statements is examined. Chapters 7, 8, and 9 deal with the church as the body and reminder of Jesus Christ, and its mission in our time, the twenty-first century.

The final chapter, "The End? The Beginning? Or the End of the Beginning?" returns to the theme that God continues to act in history and continues to call people to be the church in ways that are both old and always new.

No reflection on what it means to be the church, God's people struggling to follow Jesus Christ in the twenty-first century, can ignore what happened on September 11, 2001. Since that day's attacks on the World Trade Center and the Pentagon and the crash of a plane in Pennsylvania, the world has become a different place. At the very least, the events of that fateful day reminded us that much of what we Western Christians assumed about the world and our place in it had already definitively and dramatically changed. Suddenly, religion and worldviews other than our comfortable Judeo-Christian tradition came into dramatic focus. Relationships with people of other cultures and religions immediately became critical, as did the challenge of maintaining our faith and our community in ways that are peaceful and just and compassionate.

Who will ever forget the way people turned to the church after the events of 9/11—members, adherents, friends, some getting in their cars and driving all day to be together in the church to sing, "O God, our help in ages past, our hope for years to come," to be reminded that God loves the world, that God's kingdom is both here and always coming, and that believers have nothing ultimately to fear? An interfaith service in which I was privileged to participate was sponsored by our neighboring synagogue, the Roman Catholic cathedral, and our Presbyterian church. At the end of the service, Rabbi Michael Sternfield invited the congregation—which filled every pew and extra seat, standing in the aisles, narthex, and on the front steps—to pray together, out loud, each in his or her own tradition. I will never forget the sound of those prayers: Muslim, Jewish, Christian, filling the sanctuary, rising to the one God and creator of us all.

The new world since 9/11 is the context in which the church will live and struggle to be faithful. It makes our story, the story of God's people, even more critical and fascinating.

This book is written out of my lifelong, deepening gratitude for the church and my lifelong impatience for the church to be what God calls it to be. I am grateful for the congregation that baptized, nurtured, and challenged me: the Broad Avenue Presbyterian Church of Altoona, Pennsylvania. And I am ever grateful for the congregations that called me to be their pastor and taught me what it means to be church: the Presbyterian Church of Dyer, Indiana; Bethany Presbyterian Church of Lafayette, Indiana; Broad Street Presbyterian Church of Columbus, Ohio; and the Fourth Presbyterian Church of Chicago.

Finally, I am grateful for my wife, Sue, and my five children and their spouses, all of whom have enough commitment to and impatience with the church to give me hope for the future. To them—one of whom once said, "Don't ever ask Dad a question unless you have a lot of time. He always begins with the Roman Empire and works his way up to the twenty-first century, slowly"—I dedicate this book.

1

Looking Backward and Forward

We are who we are. We began as modestly as it is possible to begin, in a rough stable, behind a Bethlehem inn. We grew steadily and then quickly we became the religion of Rome. We took for ourselves the mantle and the reality of Roman power when the empire itself began to decline. We lived in monasteries and reform movements through a one-thousand-year period sometimes known as the Middle Ages. We were part of a huge upheaval in Western history called Reformation/Renaissance/Enlightenment. We spread westward into the New World and penetrated deeply to the heart of the new societies, nations, and cultures that are still emerging in North America and South America. And we continued to extend, in the past two centuries, into all the world.

What a fascinating time to think about the church. What a challenging time to be the church. In the United States of America, there is so much change happening in the life of the church that a cottage industry of analysts, sociologists of religion, historians, and preachers has risen up to write books about it.

For one thing, the older, traditional, American churches are declining in numerical strength. Described as "mainline churches" because of their early predominance in North America along the main line of the Pennsylvania Railroad moving west from Philadelphia, the Presbyterian, Episcopal, Congregational, Methodist, and American Baptist denominations were part of the early American experience; grew and prospered along with the nation; and, over the years, exerted powerful influence politically, socially, and ethically in American culture. Sociologists observe how economic prosperity and social acceptance were reflected in one's belonging to one of the mainline churches. Most presidents and U.S. senators belonged to the Episcopal, Presbyterian, or one of the other mainline denominations. Leaders of the mainline denominations were treated as celebrities by the American press. Internally, the mainline churches prospered after the Second World War. New churches were organized, new mission programs initiated, and each of the denominations, in their social pronouncements, spoke prophetically to the body politic. It was, historians observe, almost as if the mainline denominations, collectively, were the established church of the United States.

Then something happened that continues to puzzle students of church history. Waves of post–World War II immigrants accentuated the nation's cultural, racial, and religious diversity. Never an actual majority in the United States, the mainline became a noticeable minority. In addition to the traditional strength of the Roman Catholic Church, suddenly the Southern Baptists, Mormons, and Pentecostals became significantly stronger and more visible in American life. A Southern Baptist president, Jimmy Carter, acknowledged that he had been "born again," and suddenly the evangelical churches began to emerge as powerful forces in American culture.

The numerical decline of the mainline church was surely aided by a falling birth rate: sometime in the middle of the twentieth century the birth rate within the mainline churches dropped below two, and mainliners were no longer replacing themselves with their own children. In addition, denominational labels became less important to American people. Surveys continued to reveal that American churchgoers choose their church home on the basis of factors other than denominational affiliation: the choir, preacher, building, youth program. Churchgoers started to act like consumers, and many chose churches outside the traditional mainline.

The national decline of the mainline churches is an important factor at the beginning of the twenty-first century. Some believe that the decline in numbers is a prelude to a spiritual and missional renewal. Others think that our decline is preface to our demise, that this is the post-Christian era. And beneath it all in our culture is a deepening secularism: a general sense that life is lived without God, that faith is unimportant, religion irrelevant, and the church unnecessary.

Yet there is a spiritual explosion happening in Asia, South America, and Africa. The Korean Presbyterian Church continues to grow in numbers and influence in Korean society and is aggressively sending missionaries throughout the world. South America is experiencing an extraordinary growth in Pentecostalism and in the older, missionary mainline churches. Presbyterian churches in Brazil send missionaries to Portuguese-speaking people in the United States. In East Africa, one of the most difficult and dangerous places in the world at the beginning of the century, Christian churches are growing so dramatically that there is a desperate need for leadership training, theology/education, schools, and church buildings to accommodate the newly baptized Christians.

Within the United States the startling appearance and continued growth of megachurches—churches with thousands of members, corporate-sized staffs, huge buildings, and impressive spiritual growth and community service programs—belie the suggestion that we are becoming a secular people. And throughout the culture—in books, motion pictures, and popular music—the themes of God, meaning, purpose, suffering, and hope continue to find expression.

The major issues facing American culture are either religious in nature or have major religious implications. They are, thus, issues for the church as well. Many of them are controversial and divisive. Christians of goodwill disagree on them. None of them is simple.

Letter to a Man in the Fire, the title of a book by a prominent American novelist, puts it clearly: "Does God Exist and Does He Care?"[1] The mid-twentieth century was stunned by Russian cosmonaut Yuri Gagarin's statement, after returning from the first human journey into space, that he had seen the heavens and had found no God there. Gagarin's theological naiveté was apparent to thoughtful people, but his observations did seem to punctuate the fact that modern men and women live in a world very different from the comfortable and orderly cosmos inhabited by everyone before them. If God is not in the heavens, if heaven is not a *place,* for that matter, where is God?

As the twentieth century began, the fledgling discipline of psychotherapy suggested that the very idea of God was a projection of the human need for a controlling parent figure. The philosophers agreed, and from 1914 to 1945 the world suffered two devastating wars, including the demonic effort of a state to eliminate all Jews. World War I, World War II, and the Holocaust seemed to confirm the suggestion that God is either nonexistent or radically and mysteriously absent from human affairs.

By the 1960s, theology itself was reexamining its fundamental premises in the "Death of God" movement. A *Time* magazine cover at Easter asked, "Is God Dead?"[2]

The basic questions of God—Who is God? What is God like? How does God relate to human history and to individual human beings?— continue to occupy the thinking not only of our best and brightest scholars, but also ordinary men and women who want to make sense out of their lives, and who will look to the church for support, education, and resources.

The Science Question

The twentieth century began in the aftermath of the challenge to biblical authority contained in the evolution theories of Charles Darwin. Science continued to push back the frontiers of knowledge in that century with deep space probes but also with the discovery of the microworld of the basic unit of matter: the quark, a thousand times tinier than anyone suspected. Many major diseases that had been the scourge of history in the regular appearance of plagues and pestilences were brought under control and eliminated. In full confidence, some scientists announced that human beings were about to gain all the knowledge there is. There would be no more unknown, no more mystery. Therefore, in a world where everything is understood, what reason is there for religion, for faith?

But as a new century began, science was changing its worldview once again. A worldwide epidemic of AIDS, not unlike the plagues of the Middle Ages, has reminded us that disease has not been eliminated. Mystery has reappeared. Modern science now understands that the more we learn about the universe, the more there is to learn. The universe, it turns out, is not as predictable as we thought. Matter itself is mysterious. Some scientists even sound like theologians in their expressions of awe at the magnificent mystery of the created order.

The new century heralds new, promising, and threatening conversations between science and religion. Some of those conversations will happen in the church.

The Moral Question

Probably no topic divides Christians as deeply as morality. What is good? What is moral behavior? What is specifically Christian moral behavior? The cultural revolution of the 1960s celebrated the freedom and autonomy of the individual to move beyond the strictures of convention—in music, art, career choice, education, family relationships, and sexual behavior. Christian ethicists joined the conversation, and Christian people began to disagree about what constitutes Christ-like moral behavior. As society afforded individuals new opportunities for self-determination—the opportunity to end a pregnancy by abortion, for instance—the church struggled, and continues to struggle, to discern the mind of Christ in light of the new situation in which we find ourselves. In this new century, all the churches are engaged in important conversations, and sometimes conflicts, over the issue of homosexuality and whether or not consensual, committed, same-sex relationships are included in appropriate Christian morality.

Medical science alone is presenting our society with a full complement of ethical dilemmas: the use of human embryos for stem cell research, genetic engineering, cloning, intentional termination of pregnancy, and end-of-life issues. In each of these areas medical technology has created new opportunities, new responsibilities, and new moral quandaries. Is it appropriate to tamper with the basic genetic building blocks of our humanity? If so, under what conditions, and who will be responsible for making decisions? Is it appropriate to terminate a pregnancy? Is the decision purely personal, or does it also involve society as a whole? Who shall decide how much technology and resources are appropriate to invest to prolong life when critical and incurable illnesses are present? Modern women and men will have to wrestle with these and other new issues created by continuing scientific progress, and they will look to their churches for wisdom, support, and assistance.

Remember the Past, Keep Faith with the Present, Face the Future in Confidence

Five and one-half centuries before Christ, God's people were living in a very treacherous time and place. The Babylonians had defeated the armies of Judah and carried off the leaders of the people into exile in Babylon. The captive community lived in a strange and foreign land for several generations and endured the hardships, suffering, and persecution that are the lot of displaced persons and refugees in every age. Particularly painful was the sense of loss of God's protective covenant.

> By the rivers of Babylon—
>   there we sat down and there we wept
>   when we remembered Zion. . . .
> How could we sing the LORD's song
>   in a foreign land?
>
> (Ps. 137:1, 4)

The situation was so desperately threatening that many of the people concluded that God was either nonexistent or irrelevant, that their faith and trust in God were no longer possible, and that the existence of the tradition and their own life as God's people was about to disappear as they were absorbed into the cultures of their captives.

But then, from the remaining community back in the rubble of Jerusalem came a letter reminding them that their God was not only still alive, but actually involved in the sometimes threatening events of history. It turned out to be a life-saving reminder, and it is perhaps the most relevant word of God for the church in the early years of a new century.

> Do not remember the former things,
>   or consider the things of old.
> I am about to do a new thing;
>   now it springs forth, do you not perceive it?
> (Isa. 43:18–19)

The one thing we can know for sure about the future and the future of the church is that God will be part of it and that God will be actively creating a new future for God's people. The task before us, therefore, is not unlike the challenges facing God's captive people in Babylon: to remember the past, to keep faith with the present, and to face the future with confidence, watching and listening for the new thing that God is doing.

2

Behold, a Very Old Thing

Is the church really necessary?
Religion is about God and me, isn't it? It's personal and
private. I'm a believer, I pray every day. I just don't see
what the church has to do with it.

The spiritual tenor at the beginning of the twenty-first century
is best described as radical individualism. Two dynamics illus-
trate this "spiritual individualism": a new and growing interest
in personal spirituality, personal spiritual growth, and in evangelical circles, a "personal relationship with Jesus Christ," and
at the same time, a declining interest in and commitment to the
institutional church, particularly traditional mainline churches.

Sociological studies investigate this interesting phenomenon. Robert Bellah in *Habits of the Heart* documented this new
focus on individual spirituality in hundreds of interviews and
gave it a name: "Sheilaism." One of Bellah's interviewees, a
young woman by the name of Sheila, put it this way: "I believe
in God. I'm not a religious fanatic. I can't remember the last
time I went to church. My faith has carried me a long way. It's
Sheilaism. Just my own little voice."[1]

Wade Clark Roof, the J. F. Rowny Professor of Religion and
Society at the University of California, Santa Barbara, has produced a number of important sociological analyses of modern
American religious experience, including *A Generation of Seekers: The Spiritual Journeys of the Baby Boom Generation*. Roof
wrote:

This is a generation of seekers. Diverse as they are—from Christian fundamentalists to radical feminists, from New Age explorers to get-rich-quick MBAs—baby boomers have found that they have to discover for themselves what gives their lives meaning, what values to live by. Not since the cataclysm of World War II have most of us been able simply to adopt meanings and values handed down by our parents' religion, our ethnic heritage, our nationality. Rather, what really matters became a question of personal choice and experience. . . . They value experience over beliefs, distrust institutions and leaders, stress personal fulfillment yet yearn for community, and are fluid in their allegiances—a new, truly distinct, and rather mysterious generation.[2]

They are *seekers*, not *joiners*.

The practical impact of radical "spiritual individualism" has been to shift the focus and energy of religion away from the community and the world to the individual. In the appropriate effort to remind people that Jesus did call his followers to love their neighbors as they loved themselves, modern religion has overcompensated and stressed self-love, self-affirmation, self-acceptance at the cost of the sacrificial love of neighbor and world, which is the first half of the biblical equation. The result sometimes appears to be "religion as therapy," which focuses exclusively on the individual's health, welfare, satisfaction, and salvation. Some of the most popular new liturgies and religious music focus exclusively on an individual, personal relationship with Jesus, without mention of other people, particularly neighbors in need.

There are, of course, many reasons for the numerical decline in mainline religion, but chief among them is surely the new "spiritual individualism" and antipathy toward religious institutions evident in American culture. Consequently, all churches are reevaluating their theological, programmatic and missional focus and asking whether or not the churches have missed a basic and urgent human need for personal religion. New theological studies are recovering the personal dimension of Jesus' ministry and teachings, and rediscovering the history of deep personal piety within all the churches' traditions.

But the question remains near the surface of our culture. Is the church really necessary? After all, a vast distance, not only in terms of years, exists between the teachings of Jesus and the monumental and complex reality of the Vatican. There is a vast difference between the straightforward life of discipleship described in the Gospels and the machinations of the Central Committee of the World Council of Churches, or the national governing boards, councils, and general assemblies of the denominations. First-time visitors to St. Peter's in Rome, or the Presbyterian Center in Louisville, or a meeting of the General Assembly often find themselves quietly asking, "What does all this have to do with Jesus?"

So, let's go back to the beginning and ask the basic question: Is the church really necessary? Another approach is to question, "Why is there a church in the first place?"

The answer takes us all the way back to the beginning, literally all the way back to the heart of God.

From its outset the Bible tells a story about a community of people. In ways that are subtle and not so subtle, the biblical narrative is not only about God, but also about God's people and, most importantly, their relationship with God and with one another. As a matter of fact, this emphasis on God—in relationship with people—and the creation of a special community of God's people is what is unique about the Hebrew Scriptures. The Bible is not an abstract philosophic tome full of ideas, concepts, and propositions about the nature of God. The way the Bible talks about God is by telling stories about God's people: how the people obey/disobey God, and how they are faithful/unfaithful, heroic/cowardly, honest/dishonest, loving/hateful, compassionate/uncaring, just/unjust. Mostly the Bible tells the remarkable story of how deeply and strongly God loves the people, and how patient and kind and merciful God is in relationship with the people, how faithful God is to the people, even when they are unfaithful.

It's almost as if God chooses to be God through the life of the people, a dynamic that is present from the very beginning of the story.

Poet James Weldon Johnson has seen and winsomely conveyed this important biblical truth:

And God stepped out on space,
And He looked around and said,
"I'm lonely—
I'll make me a world." . . .
Then God walked around
And God looked around
On all that He had made.
He looked at His moon,
And He looked at His little stars;
He looked on His world
With all its living things,
And God said, *"I'm lonely still."*

Then God sat down
On the side of a hill where He could think;
By a deep, wide river He sat down;
With His head in His hands,
God thought and thought,
Till He thought, *"I'll make me a man!"*

Up from the bed of the river
God scooped the clay;
And by the bank of the river
He kneeled Him down;
And there the great God almighty,
Who lit the sun and fixed it in the sky,
Who flung the stars to the most far corner of the night,
Who rounded the earth in the middle of His hand—
This Great God,
Like a mammy bending over her baby,
Kneeled down in the dust
Toiling over a lump of clay
Till He shaped it in His own image;

Then into it He blew the breath of life,
And man became a living soul.[3]

God created the world because God's love naturally reaches out to
include others—plants, animals, even us. It is just like God to create

life. Another way of putting it is that God's love needs someone to love, and so God creates someone who will be the recipient of God's love and will reciprocate by faithfully loving God, and who will reflect God's love in relationship with other people in the life of the human community.

God carefully fashions a man and woman, and unlike the other animals and plants and rocks and water and mountains, the human creatures are capable of relationship with God. Adam—man, Eve—woman, can hear God speak, can have a conversation with God, and are given the privilege of the garden and the responsibility for its maintenance. Even on its very first page, the Bible talks about God by talking about the human community.

The other thing about human beings, the Bible says, is that they have the power and the unfortunate tendency to ignore one another and in the process destroy the precious gift of community. Adam and Eve refuse to abide by the basic rules of the garden paradise, are driven out of Eden and into human history, and not long after experience the brokenness of the human condition/community, as their oldest son murders his brother.

But even in the midst of the tragedy precipitated by their own disobedience, God continues to love the man and woman, lovingly fashioning clothing for them as they leave the security of the garden paradise (Gen. 3:23).

In a series of covenants, first with Noah, then with Abraham, God continues to create a community of people: "I will make of you a great nation, and I will bless you, and make your name great, so that you will be a blessing" (Gen. 12:2). God needs a community of people apparently, not only to receive blessing, but to be a blessing to the nations. God's people have privilege and responsibility, simultaneously and equally. God's people, on the other hand, being people, are not consistently happy with either their privilege or responsibilities and consistently fail to live up to God's expectations and hopes for them. The community is in constant danger of disintegration, but God is patiently faithful, even though in more than one incident God's exasperation and anger are kindled.

When the people are led out of their slavery in Egypt by Moses, they have barely escaped the pursuing Egyptian army at the Red Sea, when they start to complain, grumble, argue: "If only we had died by the hand of the LORD in the land of Egypt, when we sat by the flesh-pots and ate our fill of bread; for you have brought us out into this wilderness to kill this whole assembly with hunger" (Exod. 16:3).

But God is patient. God provides water and bread, a pillar of fire at night and a cloud by day to guide the people through the wilderness. And when they arrive at a mountain called Sinai, the separate tribes of Israel become a people, a community, a nation, as Moses, their leader, receives the ten fundamental laws to guide and regulate their life together. The Ten Commandments, a gift from God, are the basic rules by which God's people will live together in a way that will allow them to "be a blessing."

In some ways the Bible is the story of the amazing patience of God with a people who do not do much to deserve God's love. Centuries after the experiences in the wilderness (the exodus), God's people are breaking every commandment in sight, ignoring the plight of their own poor and marginalized. The community is threatened by economic injustice—the rich get richer while the poor get poorer. Conspicuous consumption has made a sham of the community's solidarity. Worst of all, the people are flirting with other deities, straying from the fundamental monotheism that is at the very heart of their life.

At just the right moment two brave men call the people to account. The prophet Amos reminds them that God has expectations, that the community is failing miserably to live up to them:

> You only have I known
>   of all the families of the earth;
> therefore I will punish you
>   for all your iniquities.
> (Amos 3:2)

Amos is not exactly delicate in pointing out the community's failures:

> Hear this word, you cows of Bashan . . .
> who oppress the poor, who crush the needy.
> (Amos 4:1)

But even as Amos predicts the disasters that will occur because of the community's unfaithfulness, he remembers God's amazing patience and love, God's commitment to the people:

> I will restore the fortunes of my people Israel,
>   and they shall rebuild the ruined cities and inhabit them.
>
>   (Amos 9:14)

God is hopelessly in love with the people and will not abandon them. One of the high points in the history of human thought about God comes from the prophet Hosea, who describes the nation as an unfaithful wife and God as her devastated husband whose love overcomes resentment, revenge, hurt, betrayal—a love that literally conquers all:

> How can I give you up, Ephraim?
>   How can I hand you over, O Israel? . . .
> My heart recoils within me;
>   my compassion grows warm and tender.
> I will not execute my fierce anger. . . .
>   (Hos. 11:8–9)

A Community Created in Bondage and Exile

Individual people become a community in the frightening experiences of their history. They preserve the memory of their escape from slavery, their wandering in the wilderness, the giving of the law at Mount Sinai, their conquest and occupation of the land by retelling and reenacting the events in annual liturgical celebrations, festivals, and liturgies. Their religious worship reminds them of who their God is, but also who they are as God's people.

Along with the exodus, the other event that creates the community of God's people is the exile and Babylonian captivity. In the sixth century BC, the two entities of the people of God—Israel in the north, Judah in the south—are defeated disastrously and utterly. The conquering Babylonians devise a clever strategy to end, once and for all, the existence of the community. It was a particularly ingenious form of ethnic cleansing called cultural assimilation. Many of the people, including the nation's political, cultural, and religious leadership, were removed from Judah and taken to Babylon and held captive. So far as we know, the Babylonian exiles were invited to become Babylonians, adopt Babylonian customs, worship Babylonian gods. The effectiveness of the strategy is evidenced in the poignancy of the literature that the homesick and discouraged exiles produced:

> By the rivers of Babylon—
>   there we sat down and there we wept
>   when we remembered Zion.
> On the willows there
>   we hung up our harps. . . .
> How could we sing the LORD's song
>   in a foreign land?
>
> (Ps. 137:1–2, 4)

And, again, a prophetic voice is raised to remind the people of God's commitment to their community. God has not forgotten! God will be faithful!

> Comfort, O comfort, my people,
>   says your God.
> Speak tenderly to Jerusalem
>   and cry to her
> that she has served her term. . . .
> A voice cries out,
>   "In the wilderness prepare the way of the LORD,
>   make straight in the desert a highway for our God."
>
> (Isa. 40:1–3)

The eloquent poet whose words are found in Isaiah 40–55, sometimes called "Second Isaiah," reminded the people that God had not forgotten, that they were going home again, and that they had a job to do—a mission.

> Thus says God, the LORD . . .
>   I have taken you by the hand and kept you;
> I have given you as a convenant to the people,
>   a light to the nations,
>   to open the eyes that are blind,
> to bring out the prisoners from the dungeon. . . .
> See, the former things have come to pass,
>   and new things I now declare.
>
> (Isa. 42:5, 6b, 7, 9)

It is impossible to read these words from the sixth century BC and not think of one of those people of God, a member of that community, the Palestinian Jew, Jesus of Nazareth and the community of people who for two thousand years have claimed his name. It is impossible to read what the prophet wrote about the people and their mission,

> Surely he has borne our infirmities. . . .
> He was wounded for our transgressions,
>   crushed for our iniquities;
> upon him was the punishment that made us whole,
> and by his bruises we are healed.
>
> (Isa. 53:4–5),

and not think of the life, ministry, and death of Jesus of Nazareth, whom we know as the Christ, God's Messiah.

It is impossible to read what Isaiah said about the mission of the people of God, to be

> a light to the nations,
>   to open the eyes that are blind,
>   to bring out the prisoners from the dungeon . . .
>
> (Isa. 42:7),

and not be reminded of the church of Jesus Christ and its mission in the world, and God's continuing commitment to the blessed community, the people of God.

It has been said that there is no such thing as a solitary Jew. The great gifts of Judaism are monotheism, the singleness and oneness of God, and the unique conclusion that every human being is created in the image of God and therefore has both dignity and responsibility to be God's partner in creation. From these factors emerged the community of God's people who know God's oneness, who have experienced God's love and faithfulness, who have been forgiven and restored, and whose life together as a people, a community, a nation, reflects their experience of God. Judaism reminds us that we are all children of God, God's family, and that God expects us to love and honor every human being on earth as individuals and as a community.

The great gift of the Jews to Christians is a reminder that there can be no such thing as a solitary Christian. Christians are part of the blessed community, the people of God, a wild olive shoot, grafted onto the original tree and root, as Paul wrote (Rom. 11:17). Christians are the church.

Roman Catholic theologians have long maintained that "there is no salvation outside the church."[4] Reformed theologians, including no less than John Calvin, have agreed. Rather than consigning to heaven or hell members of a particular church, the point is that the tradition of our faith, from its very beginnings, is about the creation and mission of a people. The church is simply what happens when people accept Jesus Christ as their Lord and decide to follow him.

No, religion is not about God and me. It's about God and me and you, all of us, and our neighbors, particularly the ones who need us. Of course, my faith is personal and private, but it is also public and corporate. And the church, the church of Jesus Christ, has everything in the world to do with it.

"I Believe in the Holy Catholic Church"

What a pity, that so hard on the heels of Christ come the Christians. There is no breather. The disciples turn into the early Christians between one rushed verse and another. What a dismaying pity, that here come the Christians already, flawed to the core, full of wild ideas and self-importance. . . . They set out immediately to take over the world and they pretty much did it. They converted emperors, raised armies, lined their pockets with real money, and did evil things large and small, in century after century, including this one. They are smug and busy, just like us, and who could believe in them?[1]

*E*very Sunday in Christian congregations all over the world, otherwise reasonable men, women, and children stand up and say something unreasonable, maybe even preposterous: "I believe in the holy catholic church." The phrase is in the Apostles' Creed, one of the oldest Christian confessions, and people have been saying it for something like eighteen hundred years.

Believe in the church? Belief in the church as a basic tenet of faith, along with belief in God, Jesus Christ, the Holy Spirit, the resurrection? Who can believe in the church? It is the holy catholic church, by the way, not the Roman Catholic Church, or the Lutheran, Baptist, or Presbyterian church. "Holy" means God has more to do with it than we do, and "catholic" means universal, worldwide, a church that transcends all the labels, theologies, rituals, and rules we have attached to it: a church known to God.

How, possibly, can we believe in the church? Or to put it another way, Did Jesus intend to start a church? This question is often asked upon standing in the nave of the Basilica of St. Peter in Rome—the largest church building in the world, with the highest dome and a collection of priceless art; or after a particularly bruising debate at a meeting of the General Assembly; or during the board meeting of your congregation, during which tempers flared and individuals treated one another with something less than respect and courtesy, not to mention love. American poet Robert Frost said he had a lover's quarrel with the world.[2] People who know the church, work in their local congregation, and serve their denomination often have a lover's quarrel with their churches.

Skeptics point out that Jesus only used the term "church" (*ekklēsia* in Greek) three times in the Gospel narratives, all three in the Gospel according to Matthew. The word first occurs in the course of a dialogue between Jesus and his disciples, which happens while they are traveling near Caesarea Philippi.

> "Who do people say I am?" Jesus asks.
> "John the Baptist, Elijah, Jeremiah," the disciples respond.
> "But who do you say that I am?" Jesus asks.
> Peter answers: "You are the Messiah, the Son of the living God." (Matt. 16:13–16, paraphrased)

And then comes the church:

> Blessed are you, Simon son of Jonah! For flesh and blood has not revealed this to you, but my Father in heaven. And I tell you, you are Peter, and on this rock I will build my church, and the gates of Hades will not prevail against it. (Matt. 16:17–18)

The way Matthew tells it, Jesus goes on to give Peter some very important authority, the keys of the kingdom, and the power to bind and loose things in heaven and on earth. The Roman Catholic tradition believes that Peter passed on his exalted position as the rock on which the church is built, his ownership of the keys and his worldly and heavenly authority, to his successors, the bishops of Rome.

Critical scholarship has always suspected that this key passage was added to the text of Matthew much later by someone interested in advancing the reputation of Peter, who after all doesn't act like much of a rock later in the story. In fact, before it is over, Peter will disgrace himself by denying three times that he even knows Jesus.

Whether Jesus intended the Vatican, the Presbyterian Church (U.S.A.), or the literally thousands of denominations and millions of congregations throughout the world, he surely did mold his little band of followers into a unique community. As they followed him through Galilee—teaching in the synagogues, healing the sick, receiving the old and the young, eating and drinking with rich and poor, respectable community leaders, and social outcasts—his followers not only found that their personal beliefs and faith and relationship with God were being transformed, but their relationship with one another was deepening as well.

For three years this small community of men and women followed and watched and listened. Jesus spent time mentoring and teaching them. The Sermon on the Mount, the beautiful collection of his teachings found in Matthew 5–7, is for them, for their edification and spiritual growth, for their life together and their life in the world as his followers, his people, his church.

> When Jesus saw the crowds, he went up the mountain, and after he sat down, his disciples came to him. Then he began to speak, and taught them, saying: Blessed are the poor in spirit. . . . You are the salt of the earth. . . . You have heard that it was said . . . , but I say to you . . . Pray then in this way: Our Father in heaven, hallowed be your name. . . . (Matt. 5:1–3, 13, 21, 22; 6:9)

Later he sent them out, two by two, to tell the story and to heal the sick. He led them from the safety of Galilee to the dangers of Jerusalem at Passover, and they watched, in amazement and fear, as crowds of people waved palm branches and welcomed him as a conquering hero. And as the end drew near, in that week we know as Holy Week, he carefully arranged for them to eat a final meal, a Last Supper, together.

That was the occasion when their belonging to him and to one another was sealed, seared into their memories, in two unforgettable acts. First, he washed their feet. Second, he broke bread, poured the cup of wine, and passed it to them with the words: "This is my body; this is my blood, eat this bread, drink this cup, in remembrance of me."

He was building his church.

They watched in horror as a net of intrigue and conspiracy closed around him. They watched from a distance as the Roman authorities agreed to his execution for sedition. They all fled in fear as he died. And they hid together in a room in Jerusalem following his burial. They were together on the first day of the week when the women returned from the tomb with their unexpected, incredible announcement that he was alive, risen from the dead. They were together in that same room when they experienced his risen presence, and together they heard his blessing and his commission, "Do not be afraid: go and tell my brothers [and sisters] to go to Galilee: there they will see me" (Matt. 28:10).

Did Jesus intend the church? The answer is that Jesus very carefully formed a community of women and men, taught them, nurtured them, loved them, and prepared them to carry on after he was gone. That community he left behind was the infant church. He gave it a job to do: "Go therefore and make disciples of all nations" (Matt. 28:19). As he expressed the reality of God in his life on earth, so the church, by what it did and what it was, would reflect the reality and truth and goodness of his life. The world would know him, Jesus Christ, down through the ages, because of the church.

He said it beautifully, after he had washed their feet at the table of the Last Supper: "I give you a new commandment, that you love one another. Just as I have loved you, you also should love one another. By this everyone will know that you are my disciples, if you have love for one another" (John 13:34–35).

After his death and resurrection, the disciples remained in Jerusalem, still hiding from the authorities who might have been inclined to crucify them for their association with him. And then the most unlikely thing happened, given their tendency to flee at the first sign of danger. They were still together on the Jewish feast day of Pentecost. Together the disciples experienced the presence of God's spirit, and when they later tried to describe it they used dramatic metaphors—"a sound like the rush of a violent wind . . . tongues, as of fire"—and most remarkable of all, "devout Jews from every nation, . . . each one heard them speaking in the native language of each" (Acts 2:2, 3, 5, 6). The first public experience of the disciples after the resurrection was an experience of power and communication. Fearful disciples, hiding in a room for weeks, suddenly stood up and publicly declared their faith in Jesus Christ. Peter, last seen denying that he even knew Jesus, on Pentecost conspicuously proclaims the good news of God's love revealed in the life, death, and resurrection of Jesus. People understand. People are moved and transformed by his preaching. Three thousand people were added to their numbers (Acts 2:1–41).

The public church was born on Pentecost. Fearful disciples were transformed into brave witnesses, able to communicate with eloquence the truth of Jesus Christ. The results were dramatic and visible!

> Awe came upon everyone, because many wonders and signs were being done by the apostles. All who believed were together and had all things in common; they would sell their possessions and goods and distribute the proceeds to all, as any had need. Day by day, as they spent much time together in the temple, they broke bread at home and ate their food with glad and generous hearts, praising God and having the goodwill of all people. And day by day the Lord added to their number those who were being saved. (Acts 2:43–47)

The church began in the heart of God, in the covenants God made with a people. The infant church took its first steps when Jesus called men and women to follow him and then taught them how to live as his disciples. The church exploded into human history on the day of Pentecost when the good news of Jesus was proclaimed in the public square and people responded, were transformed, and joined the movement.

People from every nation became followers of Jesus that day in Jerusalem. And it wasn't long until the Jesus movement was spreading throughout the towns and villages of Judea, Galilee, Samaria. Boldly and publicly his followers were declaring that he was the Son of God, the one long promised, the Messiah—"Christos" in Greek. They began to call him Jesus the Christ, and they began to identify themselves with him. Others called them Christians.

No more than two decades after his death and resurrection, the followers of Jesus began a process of differentiation and separation from the Temple in Jerusalem and Judaism. The new Christians were Jews. They met in synagogues, read Hebrew Scripture, followed the law of Moses. But official disapproval of their new ideas, and their conviction and claim that Jesus was the Messiah, soon led to conflict and persecution. One of the most ardent persecutors, a brilliant Pharisee by the name of Saul of Tarsus, would soon change the course of human history when he, too, became a disciple of Jesus.

On a tour of archaeological wonders of Greece and Turkey, a prerequisite is a visit to the ruins of ancient Ephesus. Much of the old city is visible: the streets with chariot tracks worn deeply, the foundations and partial walls of shops, the public bathhouses and latrine, the dramatic facade of the library creatively designed to maximize the use of sunlight for reading, the great amphitheater, and etched into a paving stone a cross inside a circle and a fish, Christian symbols nearly two thousand years old. Students of history and readers of the New Testament know about the missionary journeys of Paul, the churches he established and then the letters he wrote to them. But to see this cross and the fish etched into a two-thousand-year-old paving stone is to know profoundly that they were there: the Christians, the early church.

Saul of Tarsus was a zealot about his religion. A devout Jew, a Pharisee, a Roman citizen by birth, Saul was energetic, brilliant, and passionate. He concluded, in the years following the life and death of Jesus, that Jesus and his followers were not only a nuisance, but also a threat to the integrity of the faith of Israel. Saul took it upon himself to be the defender of his faith and persuaded the Roman authorities that the followers of Jesus were guilty of the same sedition that was the charge against their executed leader. Armed with arrest warrants, Saul would descend on an unsuspecting community of believers, expose them, and arrange for their public accusation and arrest. He had earned a reputation as a fierce persecutor of the church. And then one day, on his way to Damascus to round up the Christians who were affiliated with the local synagogue, Saul's world was turned upside down. There was a brilliant light. He fell down and heard a voice, "Why are you persecuting me, Saul?" and the passionate Pharisee was unable to speak or see. When his sight returned, Saul of Tarsus had a new worldview, a new faith, a new and passionate devotion to the one he had so vigorously persecuted, and a new name: Paul. It is one of the most memorable reversals in history, and it is accurate to say about Paul that he forever changed the course of the human story.

Paul turned out to be as energetic and brilliant and innovative and passionate in the cause of Jesus Christ as he was persecuting the church. His missionary journeys were authentic and dangerous adventures, traveling by foot and by sea from Antioch through Asia Minor (modern Turkey) to Greece and back to Jerusalem and then off again to Rhodes and Crete and Malta and finally all the way to Rome. There were three missionary journeys and a fourth during which Paul was a prisoner, traveling to Rome to exercise his citizen's right of appeal to the emperor. Paul had been arrested in Jerusalem in much the same way as Jesus. Church tradition is that after a period of house arrest, Paul was executed in Rome. We know the names of the cities and towns where he preached the gospel and established churches: Corinth, Ephesus, Galatia, Philippi, Colossae, Thessalonica. Paul later wrote letters to them on a variety of topics, personal and official, about doctrinal arguments, the practices of worship, the characteristics of the new life in Christ.

The Acts of the Apostles, actually volume two of a major work written by Luke, tells the exciting story of Paul and the early church. As one reads the Acts of the Apostles in conjunction with the letters Paul and his own followers wrote, the earliest Christian church begins to come into focus.

The practice of the earliest church followed a pattern. Paul, or one of the other traveling missionary/evangelists, would arrive in a city, go to the synagogue, and because he was a Pharisee, take part in the reading and exposition of Hebrew Scripture that took place daily. That was the context for the first Christian preaching. Paul tells the story of Jesus, how Jesus of Nazareth was the fulfillment of the ancient promise, God's Messiah. Some Jews and God-fearing Gentiles—non-Jews who were intrigued with the monotheism and high moral content of Judaism and the synagogue—heard and believed. For a while the new movement lived comfortably within Judaism. But conflict was inevitable, and soon, in city after city, the followers of Jesus pulled away from the synagogue and began to meet privately, in one another's homes.

Because they still saw themselves as part of Judaism, they met on the Sabbath eve for a common meal, following Jesus' own instruction to share the bread and cup in remembrance of him. It was an inclusive fellowship apparently. Women and children were welcome, as were outcasts and marginal people who were not welcome elsewhere in society. They brought food to share, not unlike a modern church potluck supper. They sang hymns. They read whatever letters Paul or some other missionary may have written. They prayed. And they took bread and shared the cup in memory of Jesus. When visitors wanted to join the fellowship, they used an ancient rite of Judaism that Jesus himself had experienced: baptism. They eventually called themselves Christians, and to describe the new body they were becoming, they began to use a Greek word, *ekklēsia*, which means "those who are called out." We translate *ekklēsia* as "church."

Their care for one another was conspicuous. They not only proclaimed publicly their faith in Jesus Christ, they lived it. People saw how they lived and were attracted to the new movement. And they argued about all the issues about which Christians still argue: doctrine, right practice, morality, power, and authority. On occasion their conflicts became so public that Paul addressed them directly. In 1 Corinthians, Paul scolds, pleads, and finally calls them to show the world a "more excellent way" (1 Cor. 12:31), the way of love.

And they organized. First they established the office of deacon to care for the widows and orphans among them and to distribute the leftover food from their Friday evening dinner, now known as love feasts. Next they created an office to bear responsibility for the life of the church. They used the Greek word *presbyteros* to designate the new leadership position. We translate *presbyteros* "elder" or "bishop."

By the end of the first century AD, seventy years after Jesus, the church had spread throughout the empire and all the way to the capital city of Rome. Its adherents were mostly from the bottom strata of Roman culture: poor people, slaves, outcasts, women. But increasingly people of means and influence were attracted to the gospel as well.

Two major issues dominated and threatened the life of the early church. The first was the question of how a person qualified to be a member of the church. It is the same issue of inclusiveness/exclusiveness that challenges the church of the twenty-first century. In the first century, the original followers of Jesus were Jews. Jesus himself was a Jew. He learned the psalms and Hebrew Scriptures in the synagogue school and by attending services with his father and the other men of Nazareth. He knew the Law and Prophets. He visited the Temple in Jerusalem as a boy, and as he died he quoted from memory a Hebrew prayer, "My God, why have you forsaken me?" (Ps. 22). His disciples were all Jews. There is no evidence that the first Christians found any difficulty combining the new way of Jesus with their traditional Jewish religious practices.

But as the church spread north and west from Jerusalem and Galilee, to the cities of the empire, Gentiles began to be attracted. At first everyone assumed that a new convert to Christianity needed first to become Jewish, to adhere to the law of Moses, including, for men, the rite of circumcision. More important, however, was the issue of how one becomes a Christian, a member of the Christian church. Paul had become convinced, out of his own experience, that God's saving love in Jesus Christ came as a gift and that the only possible human response was faith. You could not earn your way into the church by good deeds, following the law, or submitting to circumcision. Paul and his followers were inclined to accept Gentiles as church members. The older church in Jerusalem held out for the more conservative position, requiring converts to adhere to the law of Moses. The issue was argued heatedly throughout the new churches. The Jerusalem party even sent delegations to travel to the new churches to advocate for and enforce the conservative positions. Finally, a council of church leaders was called in Jerusalem (see Acts 10–11). Peter, who had baptized a Gentile Roman centurion from Caesarea by the name of Cornelius, reported to the council and described a dream in which God had shown him that the gospel was for everyone, Jew and Gentile, slave and free, male and female. The council of leaders was persuaded by Peter's experience, and the church broadened its vision and its mission in the world.

The second challenge to the early church came in the form of persecution. Not everyone in Rome welcomed the growth of a new religious sect, particularly one that forbade the worship of gods other than the God of Abraham, the God and Father of Jesus. Official Roman religion had multiple deities, and chief among them was the emperor himself. When Roman legions rode into town carrying a stanchion with the golden eagle on top, symbol of the empire's and the emperor's supremacy, citizens were required to bow. Christians refused. When they said, in the original creed, "Jesus is Lord," it meant "Caesar is not Lord." And so gradually at first, and then in a systematic campaign of terror and repression, Roman authority turned against the church.

Christians were harassed, humiliated, discriminated against, and finally arrested, tortured, and executed. But mysteriously, the more the church was persecuted, the stronger and more vital it became. "The blood of the martyrs is the seed of the church," said Tertullian.[3]

The story of the early Christian church is heroic and inspiring. Men and women lived and died for the new way of Jesus. They showed the world around them a new idea of God and God's will for humankind, and a new way to live with one another. They showed the world compassion and justice and sacrifice, and the world was impressed. They planted the church so deeply in the cities and towns and culture of the Roman Empire that, in three hundred years, Christianity would become the official religion of the empire.

Along the way the early Christians argued and fought with one another, were alternatively courageous and cowardly, faithful and conspicuously unfaithful. In short, they acted like the church has always acted. But they had something important going for them, namely, the promise of Jesus. It was and is, ultimately, his project, his church—not theirs or ours. And he promised that the gates of hell will not prevail against it.

4

Church, Empire, Reformation

*I*t is impossible to imagine Western civilization, not to mention American history, without the presence of Christian faith and the Christian church. But it was very different in the beginning.

The Christian church began as an underground movement among the oppressed and marginalized people in first-century culture. It was ignored, then looked upon suspiciously, and finally persecuted by the dominant culture, the people and institutions of real power and influence. Jesus had promised that his church would withstand the forces of hell itself, and that is exactly what Christians in the second and third centuries must have thought they were up against as Roman authorities arrested, tortured, and executed them in Rome's Colosseum for Saturday afternoon entertainment.

Despite the persecution of the early church mentioned in the previous chapter, the enduring miracle is that official opposition and persecution seemed to refine and strengthen the church. In a pattern that would be repeated in history—in Nazi Germany in the 1930s and 1940s, and behind the Iron Curtain and in Communist China in the 1950s, 1960s, and 1970s—the church went underground, thrived, grew, and became braver and more compelling under the fiercest and cruelest official opposition.

The greater challenge, and perhaps danger, for the church has always been the official approval and sponsorship of mainstream culture. And it began, for better or worse, when the Roman emperor himself, Constantine the Great, decided to favor Christianity and to reverse two hundred years of official opposition and persecution by declaring that it was no longer illegal to be a believer in Jesus Christ and to practice Christianity. Some historians think Constantine's mother, who had adopted the Christian religion, influenced him to soften the official stance of the imperial government. Other historians point out that the old Roman Empire was beginning to decline and come apart, and that Constantine used Christianity, a new religion growing in popularity, to hold it together. The tradition is that before a critical battle at Milvian Bridge on October 28, 312, Constantine had a vision of the cross on a Roman shield and the inscription "In hoc signo vinces [In this sign, conquer]." Constantine's legions were victorious that day, and it wasn't long before all Roman shields bore the cross of Christ, the persecutions were eased, and the church was allowed to live freely in the Roman Empire.

It is impossible to overestimate the impact of Constantine's decision. Suddenly Christians were free to be Christians publicly. The church no longer had to hide; weekly worship services could be held openly and publicly. The persecutions immediately stopped, the blood of the martyrs ceased flowing, and the Christian leaders were no longer subversive enemies of the state, but people of public stature and influence. Unlike anything in its three-hundred-year history, the church suddenly found itself able to own real estate, confer titles, and act like a public institution.

Christianity, in the brief span of three hundred years, had grown from its humble beginnings as a marginal Jewish sect to the official religion of the most powerful political entity the world had ever known. Now Roman legions carried the Christian faith and the Christian church with them as far away as northern Europe and Britain. Christian scholarship began to emerge in the great classical centers of learning as the gospel confronted classical Greek and Roman learning. Athanasius, Ambrose, Jerome, and John Chrysostom expressed and explored the gospel in the language of philosophy. Augustine of Hippo is one of the towering intellects in Western history, and his *Confessions* and *The City of God* are still regarded as high points in Western intellectual history.

The major tasks for the church in its new, favored position were to create a structure to function openly, to provide for standards and control, and to sponsor the continuing process of following Jesus' mandate to go into all the world with the gospel. The structural model that seemed most reasonable was the one everybody knew: the imperial structure of Roman government. Authority was lodged in one person at the top of a pyramid of power and distributed downward. Emperors and governors made all essential decisions for the mass of people at the bottom of the pyramid. The church already had designated its leading clergy as bishops, who exercised authority over all the churches in a geographical area. Bishops of larger cities were called Metropolitans. It was natural for the bishop of Rome, the largest and most important city of the empire, to become a leader of leaders, a father to the bishops, a *papa*, a pope.

The growth of the papacy in power, authority, and wealth through the Middle Ages is a remarkable phenomenon. Historians point out that as the Roman Empire began to decline under the unrelenting onslaught of the tribal peoples surrounding its borders, the one remaining viable structure of the older empire was the church. It is no accident that the medieval popes acted like Roman emperors and that the church took for itself all the trappings of a political state: an army, a treasury, a court system, delegates and legates and secretaries whose job it was to conduct the church's complicated relationship with the monarchies and courts of Europe. When Henry IV, holy Roman emperor, questioned papal authority, Pope Gregory VII (Hildebrand) excommunicated Henry and released all his subjects from their oaths of allegiance. "It was the boldest assertion of papal authority that had ever been made." The emperor responded by calling Hildebrand "no pope, but a false monk." The political winds favored the pope, however, and Henry traveled to the Alpine Castle of Canossa and waited, penitently, barefoot in the snow, in January 1077 for papal forgiveness and restoration of his worldly authority.[1] The influence of the papacy continued to grow, culminating in the reign of Innocent III, one of the most powerful men in the world and one of the ablest of all the popes.

By the fourteenth century, popes were being chosen for political reasons: Clement V (1305–1314) was the political puppet of the French king, Philip IV. During his reign the papacy was removed to Avignon, France, where it remained from 1309 until 1377, a period sometimes known as the Babylonian captivity of the papacy. So convoluted were the politics of papal aspirates and candidates that at one time during this period there were three claimants to the papal throne.

Jesus had created the church and promised that nothing would prevail over it. And so, from within the church itself came a critique, a counterculture movement, a reform movement. Men and women such as Anthony and Benedict saw what the church had become, the political entanglements and compromises that were necessary to maintain its public position, and decided to withdraw. The authentic Christian life, they believed, could be lived in modest, small communities, guided by basic Christ-like virtues: poverty, simplicity, and generosity. Monasteries began to spring up throughout Christendom and became an important and creative part of the medieval church. The monks and nuns in their monasteries not only reminded the rest of the church and the world of Jesus' emphasis on humility and generosity, they played an important role in the preservation of classical literature and art through what historians call the Early Middle Ages.

With the collapse of the Roman Empire and the defeat and destruction of cities, centers of learning and libraries were lost. Classical texts were protected in the monasteries, carefully copied and preserved. It was in the monasteries along the Celtic rim of the old empire in Britain and Ireland that ancient art, manuscript ornamentation, jewelry making, and poetry were preserved and practiced. One of the world's artistic treasures is the Book of Kells, a hand-copied Bible with gorgeously elaborate ornamentation on every page. The Book of Kells is on display in the library at Trinity University in Dublin. To see it is to know something of the miracle of the monastic movement.

In Italy, a privileged young military mercenary from Assisi by the name of Francis (1182–1226), compelled by the gentleness and humility of Jesus, sold his substantial possessions—to the consternation of his wealthy father—and began to live out a life of quiet prayer and reflection in harmony with all God's creatures. The Franciscans continue his legacy and witness into the twenty-first century.

Lord Acton wrote, "Power tends to corrupt: absolute power corrupts absolutely."[2] And so it was with the medieval church. The correction came in the form of a reform movement from within the church itself.

God's lively word was present in the life of the church, inspiring, agitating, moving among God's people, stirring up courageous acts of hope and renewal. Sometimes the church does not want to hear that word. Sometimes the church itself resists reformation.

John Wycliffe, an Oxford theologian, translated the Vulgate, the Latin Bible, into English and infuriated the Vatican. After his death in 1384, the pope ordered his bones dug up, crushed, and scattered. William Tyndale (1492–1536) also translated Scripture into English and was burned at the stake. Jan Hus in Bohemia (1373–1415) spoke out for laypersons and was burned at the stake for his convictions. But it was an Augustinian monk by the name of Martin Luther who ignited the conflagration that would become the Protestant Reformation. Luther was a biblical scholar and a theologian. He struggled intellectually and spiritually with the matter of his own salvation. "How is it that we are saved?" he asked. His church assured him that his salvation was guaranteed by his obedience to the church rules, standards, creeds, and obligations—salvation by works. The church taught that the saints produced more good works than they needed to provide for their own salvation, and that the excess good works could be earned and purchased. The church issued "indulgences" that, when purchased, reduced the amount of time the buyer would have to spend in purgatory. Indulgences could be purchased for persons already dead.

Luther, in the meantime, struggled with the question of his own salvation. No matter how hard he tried, no matter how often he confessed his sins or performed good works or inflicted pain on his own body, he still did not experience God's love or his own salvation. And then, in his study of Paul's Letter to the Romans, Luther discovered a truth that suddenly answered his question. "I am not ashamed of the gospel; it is the power of God for salvation to everyone who has faith. . . . 'The one who is righteous will live by faith'" (Rom. 1:16). Salvation is God's gift. It cannot be earned or purchased. The whole message of the gospel was that in Jesus Christ, God has done something for human beings that they could not do for themselves. All a recipient of God's amazing grace can do, Luther discovered, was be thankful and joyful and trust God. We are saved by grace through faith.

When a Dominican priest by the name of Tetzel visited Wittenberg, selling indulgences in the town square, Brother Martin Luther was incensed. Tetzel's sermon was compelling:

Listen now, God and St. Peter call you. Consider the salvation of your souls and those of your loved ones departed. . . . Listen

to the voices of your dear dead relatives. . . . 'Will you let us lie here in flames? Will you delay our promised glory?'
Remember that you are able to release them for

> As soon as the coin in the coffer rings
> The soul from purgatory springs.[3]

Luther responded by writing down in ninety-five theses his ideas about indulgences and salvation by faith, not works, and God's grace in Jesus Christ. According to the custom of the day, Luther nailed them to the door of the castle church, inviting anyone to debate his ideas. It was October 31, 1517, the Eve of All Saints' Day and the date that forever changed the church of Jesus Christ.

Luther wanted only to reform the church he loved, not fracture it. But once Reformation ideas were articulated publicly, they were welcomed and spread widely. Throughout Germany, the Low Countries, and France, clergy and laity alike found the new thinking compelling. The church, in the meantime, was branding Luther a heretic, burning his writings, and making him a hero among German nobility and peasants alike, who long resented the Roman church's wealth and power. Finally, Luther appeared before the holy Roman emperor at the Diet of Worms in 1521 and was ordered to recant his ideas. His response was to refuse—"Here I stand. I can do no other. God help me."[4]

Now Luther was an outlaw as well as a heretic. But with the help of sympathizers among the German princes, he escaped; hid in the fortress of Wartburg, which inspired him to write the great Protestant hymn, "A Mighty Fortress Is Our God"; and translated the Bible into German.

It was a time of anti-Semitism in northern Europe, and Luther tragically became more anti-Semitic later in his life. But his Reformation theology spread widely in academic circles. In Paris a brilliant lawyer by the name of John Calvin was fascinated by the new thinking and cast his lot with the Reformation. Along with other Protestants, Calvin had to flee for his life and, traveling through Switzerland, was persuaded to stay in Geneva where the entire city had recently adopted the Reformation. In a remarkable career in Geneva, the brilliant, scholarly Calvin wrote one of the classic masterpieces of Christian theology, *Institutes of the Christian Religion,* and worked out an entirely new form of government for the church. In his Reformed

Church, authority would come from the people, not the hierarchy. Congregations would elect their pastors and their officers. Calvin reached back into the history of the early church and recovered the idea and office of *presbyteros* (elder). Together, elders and ministers would exercise authority in the church. Other innovations followed. Worship would be conducted in the language of the people. The Lord's Table would be spread openly in worship, and all would be welcome. The psalms would be sung in joy and gratitude by the people. Calvin's energetic imagination fostered new ideas in the city of Geneva as well: public schools so people could read and understand God's word, relief agencies for the poor and needy, laws to regulate labor and commerce.

Calvin had, and continues to have, his detractors. He was a man of his age. When Servetus, a humanist who was sentenced to death by the Roman Catholic Church for denying the doctrine of the Trinity, came to Geneva, Calvin agreed to his arrest and execution by burning at the stake. Calvin could be stern and uncompromising. His doctrine of predestination, although based on his reading of Paul and Augustine, strikes modern thinkers as harsh and arrogant. His successors, the Calvinists, are often caricatured as rigidly pious, unbending, humorless moralists. But Calvin's ideas changed the church and the world. The Reformed and Presbyterian churches are the contemporary expressions of Calvinist church polity and theology. And wherever representative government, freedom of conscience, and the equality of all people warm the hearts and compel the spirits of men and women, the world is in debt to John Calvin.

What Does It Mean to Be a Protestant/Presbyterian Today?

Many of the excesses of the medieval church were corrected following the Reformation. The Council of Trent, called by Pope Paul III in 1542, initiated a Counter-Reformation within the Roman church, and even though Roman Catholics and Protestants eyed one another suspiciously for centuries, both branches of the church today affirm one another, celebrate one another's ministries and mission, and work together in thousands of communities throughout the world.

The ideas first espoused by Luther and Calvin continue to be central to the life of the church. Some of these are as follows.

The Centrality and Authority of Scripture

The Protestant Reformation recovered the critical notion of the Word of God. It is the very nature of God to communicate. God has something to say. "In the beginning was the Word, and the Word was with God, and the Word was God" is the way the Fourth Gospel introduces the story of Jesus (John 1:1). The Word—God's self-communication—is so much a part of who God is and does that John proclaims, "The Word was with God, and the Word was God." And just how does God speak? How does the Word God has for the world get itself heard? There are three ways God has communicated and continues to communicate:

1. Through the life of a people chosen, elected, and appointed to represent God and tell God's story and be a light to the rest of the world.

2. Through the life, death, resurrection, and continuing presence of One who was God's Word incarnate. "The Word became flesh," is the way the Gospel of John puts it. "We have seen his glory as of a father's only son. . . . No one has ever seen God. It is God, the only son, . . . who has made him known" (John 1:14, 18). Jesus Christ is the perfect expression of God. He is God's Word.

3. Through the pages of the Bible. The Scriptures of the Old and New Testaments contain God's word. When inquiring people read and study Scripture, discuss Scripture, and seek the Holy Spirit's guidance in interpreting Scripture, God's Word comes to them. Some people today believe that every word of the Bible is literally true even when the Bible seems to contradict what history and biology and paleontology and archaeology tell us about the world and the human race. Fundamentalism, or biblical literalism, was not an issue for the Reformers. But Luther and Calvin, as well as other Reformation leaders, were clear that the Bible contains the word of God, not magically, but because it is God's nature to communicate. Faithful people hear the word of God in the Bible when they read, study, and seek the Spirit's illuminating guidance in prayer.

What is the final authority in the church? Before the Reformation, Scripture and church tradition, equally, were the sources of final authority. Luther and Calvin insisted that Scripture alone is authoritative for the church and church tradition. While important, instructive, and inspiring, the church is prone to make mistakes and to reflect the limitations of the human beings who constitute it. "Councils do err," John Calvin said.[5] That is to say, the church can make mistakes. The church itself is guided and judged by the word of God in Scripture.

The Word in the Life of the Church

God's word is both central and authoritative in the churches of the Reformation. That conviction is expressed in many ways:

- in the emphasis on an educated ministry, trained specifically in biblical studies, languages, and biblical interpretation.
- in church education for children and adults.
- in the centrality of preaching in Reformed worship.
- in church architecture that provides for the congregation to see in order to read, and that places the pulpit and communion table prominently as the focus of public worship.

Salvation by Grace—Not Works

Martin Luther's personal struggle to experience his salvation is reflected in the lives of many people. That God should reward and love most those people who are trying hardest to be moral and upright still seems logical. That God should love and accept us apart from anything we have done or neglected to do still doesn't seem logical. That going to church and obeying the church's rules and regulations ought to earn one some standing in God's eyes still seems to make sense.

Luther did everything he could think of and everything the church told him to do to earn God's favor. But the experience that liberated him from his guilt and from a lifetime of working at the project of his own salvation was the discovery God gives us what we need, and that what God wants from us is gratitude and love lived in our lives in a way that reflects God's will for creation. The mystery of Jesus Christ on the cross, the Reformers taught, is the mystery of God's love poured out for all people, a grace that is truly amazing.

Vocation/Calling and the Priesthood of All

The Reformers recovered a very important idea that continues to have relevance in the lives of believers today: the notion of vocation. From the Latin verb "to call," *vocation* means that everyone has a calling. That idea conflicted with conventional wisdom in the Middle Ages and in our own age. Conventional wisdom has always maintained that "a calling" is what clergy have, and the rest of us are free to make our professional and career choices on the basis of economic consideration, parental expectations, and family tradition. Luther scandalized his contemporaries with his radical idea that every common shopkeeper has a vocation as holy as a priest. And so it is part of our Reformation heritage to believe that God calls all of us, not just clergy, to our life's work. God gives each of us gifts, skills and abilities that are unique, and God calls each of us to use those gifts for God's kingdom and in service to the human community. In Luther's terms, shopkeepers, homemakers, physicians, police officers, clerks, government officers, and bus drivers—each has a calling, a holy vocation.

Power to the People—Faith with Political Implications

The Reformers recovered the idea of the sanctity of the individual at a time when only the elite, the wealthy, and the powerful were regarded as important. Each of us is created in the image of God. So, the Reformers reasoned, each of us has the right to live a full life and to participate in the process by which human life is structured and governed.

These ideas sounded subversive in an age that assumed that political authority belonged not to the people, particularly poor people, but to kings and princes and the church hierarchy. Powerful people in the sixteenth century rightly understood the threat posed to their privileged position by Luther, Calvin, and the other Reformers. It is also argued that the Reformers themselves failed to understand the radical political implication of their emphasis on the individual.

Calvin's new church polity, giving to the people the right to elect their own pastors and elders, was a bold and dramatic innovation in the sixteenth century. Furthermore, the idea that elected laypersons (elders) shared responsibility and authority in the church with the clergy was a dramatic contrast to the older, traditional assignment of absolute authority to the hierarchy.

Calvin wrote a ringing defense of political liberty to church leaders and even the king of France. His ideas were discussed, studied, and spread widely in a time of Renaissance and Enlightenment that would celebrate art, literature, music, and finally, political revolution, and the God-given authority and rights of the individual.

Political scientists know that the American Revolution, the Declaration of Independence, the Constitution of the United States of America, and the Bill of Rights are, at least in part, the expression in the public arena of the theological ideas of John Calvin.

A Worldly Faith

At various times in our history, Christians have concluded that the world is so sinful that the church should distance itself as much as possible from contact with the world. Sometimes Christians have become "otherworldly," to be unencumbered by worldly concerns, focused on heaven, not earth. Some scriptural texts support this idea: Creation is fallen. The flesh is sinful and gets us into a lot of trouble. Human appetites, out of control, create unhappiness, suffering, disaster. The wages of sin is death.

But the Reformers insisted that the Christian life is lived thoroughly in the world and that the church belongs thoroughly in the world. Just as Jesus lived radically and thoroughly in his society, so his church is called to live in daily contact with the world.

Sometimes the church will get its hands dirty from its worldly life. The church will sometimes address the world and its political, economic, and social structures, yet the church is always called to live in the world.

A twentieth-century saint and martyr, Dietrich Bonhoeffer, lived out this Reformation idea and paid for it with his life. Bonhoeffer was a scholarly pastor in Germany during the rise of Nazism. His instincts were to be a pacifist and remain aloof from his nation's political ordeal. But finally he was persuaded that God called him and the church to become involved and to oppose the evils of Nazism. He helped to organize the Confessing Church in Germany, which separated from the official church in order to oppose Nazi policies and then went underground. Finally, Bonhoeffer, the gentle, scholarly pastor, became part of the plot to assassinate Adolf Hitler. It was for him an expression of his faith. The plot failed, and the conspirators, including Bonhoeffer, were arrested. Shortly before his execution, Bonhoeffer wrote from his prison cell, "It is only by living completely in this world that one learns to have faith."[6]

Martin Luther or John Calvin could not have said it better.

5

Reformation to Revolution

Modern-day citizens of Geneva sometimes don't know what to make of one of their most illustrious forebears, John Calvin. His passionate commitment to Jesus Christ, which sometimes expressed itself in what seemed like arrogance, rigidity, and intolerance, is an embarrassment to this cosmopolitan European city where much of the world comes to do its business and banking, and where many of the world's helping institutions are headquartered, including the International Red Cross and UNESCO. But a trip to Geneva is not complete without visits to the Cathedral Church of St. Peter where Calvin preached, the small auditorium where the local ministers met to study Scripture with him and where he lectured daily, the Reformation Monument, and a new Museum of the Reformation.

The monument commemorating the momentous events of the sixteenth-century Protestant Reformation and the major role John Calvin and his followers played in the history of Geneva is actually a huge wall, located near the university and adjacent to a lovely park. At the center of the wall stand larger-than-life statues of the Reformers: John Calvin; Guillaume Farel, who persuaded Calvin to settle in Geneva; Theodore Beza, his intellectual and spiritual successor; and John Knox, the leader of the Scottish Reformation.

On either side of the statues are large friezes, each portraying a moment in human history when Calvin's notion of political liberty emerged in the affairs of communities and nations. Americans are often surprised and moved to see a frieze depicting the signing of the *Mayflower* Compact by the Pilgrims on the deck of their tiny ship along with English nobles presenting a Bill of Rights to William III in 1689 and John Knox preaching from the pulpit in St. Giles' Cathedral in Edinburgh.

The Protestant Reformation initially divided into two major streams: Lutheran—whose inspiration was Martin Luther and whose geographical center was northern Germany—and Reformed or Presbyterian, led by John Calvin, located in Geneva. The leaders of the two streams knew and respected each other; representatives occasionally corresponded and met with each other. Their differences were in theological focus—Lutherans on justification by faith, Reformed/Presbyterians on God's sovereignty—and also church government and style. From the very beginning, the Reformed/Presbyterian polity—lodging authority in the church, and also the body politic, in individuals who elected elders, pastors, and representatives to govern—was the distinguishing mark of the Reformed/Presbyterian churches.

In Zurich, Huldrych Zwingli sided with the Reformation and led a complementary movement of Reformed Christianity that spread and took root in Holland and the Low Countries. The Reformed Church of America; the Christian Reformed Church; the Reformed churches of Holland, Hungary, Croatia, the Czech Republic, and South Africa; and the Waldensians in northern Italy are all part of this great Reformed tradition and share with Presbyterians a common theological heritage and democratic church polity.

American Presbyterianism traces its historical roots to Scotland and Northern Ireland. How the thinking of John Calvin came to Great Britain is the story of a strong and controversial figure by the name of John Knox.

Henry VIII, king of England (1491–1547), has been described as a "man of remarkable intellectual abilities and executive force, well read and always interested in scholastic theology, sympathetic with humanism, popular with the mass of people."[1] When Luther's writings arrived in London, Henry banned them and in response published his Assertion of the Seven Sacraments in 1521. For his faithfulness Pope Leo X conferred on Henry the honorific "Defender of the Faith." Henry married Catherine of Aragon, daughter of Ferdinand and Isabella of Spain, who bore six children, only one of whom, Mary, survived. England had never been ruled by a woman monarch. Henry and his advisors concluded he needed a male heir. Complicated negotiations and machinations, including the elevation of Henry's favorite scholar, Thomas Cranmer, to the position of archbishop of Canterbury, resulted in the annulment of Henry's marriage to Catherine, denied by Pope Clement VII but approved by Cranmer. The pope, in response, prepared a Bill of Excommunication for Henry, who in the meantime had married Anne Boleyn.

Henry was a good politician. Hostility to foreign rule and influence, and resentment of English financial support of the papacy was running high. Henry forbade all payments to Rome and ruled that henceforth all English bishops would be elected upon the king's nomination. On November 3, 1534, Parliament passed the Supremacy Act, which declared that Henry and all his successors were henceforth "the only supreme head of the Church of England." The king had separated the English church from Rome and in the process established the Anglican Church and tradition. Today churches all over the world are part of the Anglican Communion, with 76 million adherents worldwide, led by the archbishop of Canterbury. Henry would marry six times, arranging for the execution of two of his wives before Jane Seymour bore a son. Ironically, Anne Boleyn's daughter, Elizabeth, would become a beloved and effective monarch, reigning from 1558 to 1603.

Reformation thinking was first brought to Scotland by priests who had encountered the writings of Martin Luther while studying in Europe. Patrick Hamilton was burned at the stake in St. Andrew's in 1528 for teaching Reformation theology. But it was a fiery priest who literally changed the course of his nation's history.

John Knox was educated at the University of Glasgow, served for a while as chaplain to the queen, and became involved in the mounting conflict between his fellow Scots and the French. Accepting an appointment as tutor and instructor in St. Andrew's, where resentment of the Roman church and its French sponsors had deepened dramatically after the public burning of Patrick Hamilton, Knox was in the castle when it was commandeered from within by Scottish nationalists, who also murdered the hated Cardinal Beaton. When French galleys laid siege to the castle and forced its surrender, Knox was taken captive and sentenced to serve as a galley slave. It was a brutal sentence. The French ships lay in port over winter, and Knox and his fellow Scots prisoners sat chained to their oars for months in the cold, damp filth of their prison ship.

Presbyterian historian James H. Smylie observes wryly, "This punishment did nothing good for his disposition.[2]

Along with Protestant refugees from all over Europe, Knox made his way to Geneva after his release by the French. He learned from John Calvin, served as a pastor to a small English-speaking congregation, and showed his gifts as scholar, translating the Geneva Bible (1560) and writing a political/theological treatise with the arresting title *The First Blast of the Trumpet against the Monstrous Regiment of Women*, a diatribe against the Roman Catholic monarchs Mary Tudor of England and Mary of Guise, queen of Scotland. Even Calvin had misgivings about Knox's intemperance.[3]

John Knox returned to his native Scotland in 1559, and from that date until his death in 1571 he led the Scottish Reformation from his pulpit at St. Giles' Cathedral, the High Kirk of Edinburgh, and became a major force in the emergence of modern Scotland. He wrote the Scots Confession, which articulates the basis of Reformed Christianity: justification, sanctification, the authority of Scripture, church and sacraments, and church officers.

The Scottish Parliament established Knox's Presbyterianism as the national church in 1560, but provided, in the tradition of both Calvin and Knox, a degree of church independence from the authority and control of the state, a freedom simply assumed in our society today.

Knox is perhaps best known for his conflicts and vigorous confrontations with Mary, queen of Scots, who eventually resigned her throne and was exiled and executed by Elizabeth I. More importantly, Knox advocated universal education and succeeded in persuading the Scottish Parliament to provide it for all the people of Scotland. He also advocated for the poor and needy and argued that government is responsible for the welfare of all—revolutionary ideas in the sixteenth century.

A large statue of John Knox stands in the courtyard of New College, University of Edinburgh. The custom is for students to doff their caps at Knox as they pass by his statue. And so should we all who enjoy today his radical notions of personal liberty, universal education, society's responsibility for the care of the poor, and separation of church from government authority.

Scottish insistence on the independence of the kirk flared often in violent conflict. When the crown attempted to enforce an Anglican liturgy on Scotland, a riot broke out in St. Giles' Cathedral in Edinburgh. Tourists can see the plaque that marks the spot where Janet Geddes threw her stool at the clergyman who was reading from the English Prayerbook. In 1638, Scottish nobles and peasants established a national covenant to defend the integrity and authority of the Church of Scotland.

A Presbyterian Assembly at Westminster

Q. What is the chief end of man?
A. Man's chief end is to glorify God, and to enjoy him forever.

The first question and answer in the Shorter Catechism is one of the direct connections modern American Presbyterians have with their past. The wonderful grace-filled style shines through in the archaic language. In the middle of the conflicts between Scotland and England over church matters, the British Parliament called an assembly to meet at Westminster in 1643. One hundred and twenty-one commissioners gathered and deliberated for five years. Among them were some very dedicated and competent Scots Presbyterians.

The documents they produced were meant to reform the Church of England. When the Anglican Church was reestablished in England, the work of the "Westminster Divines" became the theological and ecclesiastical foundation of modern Presbyterianism. The Directory for Public Worship (1644) replaced prescribed liturgies and prayers with new guidelines that offered direction but preserved freedom. Baptism and the Lord's Supper are to be celebrated regularly, openly, and publicly, and the people's worship is to be enhanced by the singing of psalms.

The Westminster Confession of Faith was completed in 1647 along with two teaching tools, the Larger Catechism and the Shorter Catechism. Together they constitute a high and eloquent point of Reformed theology.

Northern Ireland

One of the ironic twists of history is that when Elizabeth I died, she was succeeded on the throne by James VI of Scotland, son of Mary, queen of Scots, whom Elizabeth had executed. When he assumed the throne in London, James VI became James I. Among his accomplishments was the commissioning of a new translation of the Bible, employing the best scholarship and the best English of the day. The Bible that bears his name, the King James Version, is universally recognized as one of the treasures of the English language.

James also wanted to subdue his unruly Irish subjects and provide wool for the growing English markets. His idea was to recruit equally unruly, but generally loyal Scots from the borders and send them to the north of Ireland. The settlement was called the "Ulster Plantation." The Scots immigrants brought their kirk with them, and the result still reverberates. In the six counties of Northern Ireland (of the nine counties in the ancient region of Ulster), Presbyterians constitute one-third of the population, Roman Catholics one-third, and Church of Ireland (Anglican) and other Protestants one-third. In the Republic of Ireland, the Roman Catholic population is more than 95 percent. Much of the ongoing tragedy and conflict in Northern Ireland can be understood in light of James I's Ulster Plantation, including the insistence of much of the Protestant population of Northern Ireland that ties with Great Britain be maintained at all costs, and the equally vehement insistence of the Roman Catholic portion of the Northern Ireland population on reunification with the Republic, and Catholic, south. Gratefully, recent movement on all sides promises a more hopeful and less violent future.

Presbyterianism thrived among the Scots-Irish immigrants in Ulster. The Presbyterian Church of Ireland continues to be an important institution and influence in Northern Ireland's culture.

On to America

An Ulster Scot, Francis Makemie (1658–1708), is the parent of American Presbyterianism. Born in Ramelton, Ireland, graduate of

the University of Glasgow, Makemie was ordained by the Irish Presbytery of Laggan and commissioned as a missionary to the New
World. He settled on the eastern shore of Virginia in 1683, established
churches in Virginia and Maryland, and was part of a remarkable
immigration from the Scots-Irish community in Northern Ireland to
the colonies. Perhaps as many as 250 thousand came before the War
for Independence began in 1775.

Makemie played a major role in establishing religious tolerance
and diversity in the New World. He applied for and received a license
to preach, but when he traveled from Pennsylvania to New York, Lord
Cornbury, governor of the colony, decided that his license was not
valid and forbade him to preach. Makemie decided to obey his sense
of call and his conscience, engaged in civil disobedience by preaching and conducting public worship, and was arrested and jailed for
forty-six days. Makemie was clever enough to obtain a writ of habeas
corpus and subsequently was acquitted when Cornbury failed to prove
his case.

Makemie continued to preach, teach, write, and urge his friends in
Ireland to follow him to the New World while he earned a living as a
merchant. Makemie's congregation in Rehobeth, Maryland, is still an
active church, one of the oldest in the Presbyterian Church (U.S.A.).

By 1706, there were enough Presbyterians in the colonies to form
the presbytery of Philadelphia "to consult the most proper measure for
advancing religion and propagating Christianity" in the wilderness.
Makemie was present along with a dozen or so others, including, at
the second meeting, four elders.

By 1716, the synod of Philadelphia was established to incorporate
four presbyteries, and by 1729, it was embroiled in a theological
struggle. Some in the Presbyterian family argued that ministers should
subscribe to the Westminster Confession and Catechisms. Others
argued that Jesus Christ and Scripture are the only authority. The
synod made a decision that characterizes the Presbyterian Church's
ability to accommodate diversity. It declared that Christ and Scripture
are the source and rule of Christian faith and life, and that all members of presbyteries should also affirm the Westminster Standards.
The synod, though, also provided for "scrupling"—that is, disagree-
ment with those very standards. The presbytery, or congregation, had

the right to determine which scruples or disagreements were essential and necessary standards and which were not.

From the beginning, the Presbyterian Church has understood the necessity of clearly articulating its beliefs and standards and, at the same time, honoring the conscience and integrity of fellow Presbyterians who affirm the Lordship of Christ and the authority of Scripture, but disagree on some of the particulars.

Presbyterians settled in the middle colonies of New Jersey, New York, and Pennsylvania and joined the westward migration over the Alleghenies to the frontier. Some went south through the great valleys into the Carolinas. Reformed/Presbyterian adherents in New England were Congregationalists. By the middle of the eighteenth century, the Presbyterians were a large and potent constituency throughout the colonies, calling clergymen from Ireland, Scotland, and England, and now establishing educational institutions to provide indigenous leadership.

A major spiritual upheaval, the Great Awakening, gripped the colonies. Eloquent preachers like George Whitefield (1714–1770) held great throngs of inquirers in thrall. William Tennent and his sons, William and Gilbert, established a "Log College" at Neshaminy, Pennsylvania, to train Presbyterian ministers. Jonathan Edwards (1703–1758), a New York Presbyterian serving in a Congregational church in Northampton, Massachusetts, became the first great American theologian and distinguished himself as preacher, author, and administrator. His sermon "Sinners in the Hands of an Angry God" (1741) not only warned of God's wrath but brilliantly proclaimed God's grace.

The Presbyterian Church split into two streams, Old Side and New Side, in 1741. The issues had to do with the "enthusiasm" of those inspired by the new evangelical preaching. Old Siders took a dim view of it all. New Siders thought the Old Siders were stuck in the past. The two sides lived separately until reunion in 1758.

In the meantime, Presbyterians emerged as leaders in establishing and building institutions of higher education. William Tennent's Log College moved to Princeton in 1746 and became the College of New Jersey, later Princeton University. Presbyterians were instrumental in establishing the College of Philadelphia, University of Pennsylvania, King's College, and Columbia University. Reformed zeal to evangelize Native Americans helped form Dartmouth, and Presbyterian missionaries followed the frontier into the Ohio territory, a western wilderness beyond the mountains.

Presbyterians were prominent Colonial leaders. Benjamin Franklin was a Presbyterian until he tired of the theological wrangling of the Old Side–New Side debate and became an Anglican. Physicians Benjamin Rush and John Redmon were Presbyterian elders who helped form early medical practices in Philadelphia. Rush particularly was instrumental in designing and building drainage systems for the low-lying and crowded city.

Jonathan Edwards left his Massachusetts pulpit to become president of the College of New Jersey. His daughter, Esther Burr—wife of Aaron Burr—expressed some of the best of the Presbyterians' lively tradition by engaging a tutor at the College of New Jersey in "sharp combat" on the topic of the role and rights of women.

Political ferment for independence was stirring in the colonies. Resentment over British taxation without representation erupted over the Stamp Act and resulted in the Boston Tea Party and tea boycott. Britain responded with tighter controls, which prompted deeper resentment.

Scottish clergyman John Witherspoon arrived in Philadelphia in 1768, taught moral philosophy at the College of New Jersey, and soon became its president. One of his pupils was a Virginian by the name of James Madison. Witherspoon had a deep sense of the political implications of Reformed faith and was elected to the Continental Congress. After shots were fired and blood shed at Lexington and Concord in 1775, Witherspoon and other Presbyterians were torn between commitment to peace and commitment to conscience.

Eleven Presbyterians were members of the Continental Congress that voted for Thomas Jefferson's Declaration of Independence in 1776. Witherspoon was the only clergyman to sign the document.

Not all Presbyterians supported the Patriot cause, but many did. In fact, Presbyterian partisanship for the War for Independence was so vocal that on the floor of the British Parliament, Horace Walpole said, "Cousin America has eloped with a Presbyterian parson." According to a Presbyterian historian, a British soldier described the War for Independence as nothing more than an "Irish-Scotch Presbyterian rebellion."[4]

Presbyterians fought and died and served as chaplains and, when it was over, played important leadership roles in the formation of the new nation. Some historians suggest that the founding documents of the new republic, the Constitution and the Bill of Rights, reflect a basic Calvinist understanding of the human condition: the enormous potential of human beings as the crown of God's creation, but also the reality of sin. Distinguished church historian Martin E. Marty observes that some people have called the Constitution "a thoroughly Calvinist document," because of its checks and balances and sensitivity to the human propensity to abuse political power.[5]

In the aftermath of the War for Independence, the Presbyterian Church began to see itself as a national and an American church. Presbyterian commissioners gathered in Philadelphia in 1789, were called to order by John Witherspoon, constituted themselves as a General Assembly, elected John Rodgers of the First Presbyterian Church of New York as moderator, and recorded in attendance "177 ministers, 111 probationers, 215 Congregations with ministers, and 205 vacant congregations." The assembly urged Presbyterians to "keep the unity of the Spirit in the bond of peace," corresponded ecumenically with other Reformed churches, and, in fine Presbyterian style, addressed itself to and congratulated the newly inaugurated president of the United States of America, George Washington.[6]

6

A New Church for a New World

*A*fter the Revolutionary War concluded and American independence was established, the churches found themselves in a situation quite unlike anything they had experienced before—a nation with no officially sponsored religion. Many thought that the new political experiment would fail without the support and patronage of religion. Many were sure the churches would fail in this strange new environment of liberty.

It was an imperfect freedom at first. Immigrant churches, including the Congregationalists and Presbyterians, were inclined to behave like the Old World churches from which they came, assume political privilege and authority, and exclude and discriminate against religious minorities. Rhode Island, Maryland, and Pennsylvania extended religious freedom and tolerance—and safety—early in our history, and gradually the former colonies, now "sovereign states," began to understand, appreciate, and implement Thomas Jefferson's "Lively Experiment" in religious liberty.[1]

The Presbyterians, along with the Anglicans (now American Episcopalians) and Congregationalists, were the strongest of the post–Colonial era religious groups. Almost immediately the new church began to exhibit the commitments that still characterize American Presbyterianism: representative church government and the parity of clergy and laity, education, mission, and social righteousness—a singular intent to bring the gospel of Jesus Christ into encounter with the secular society in order to bring about the reign of God, or at least a better world.

In the last decades of the eighteenth century, Presbyterians established a school for girls in New York and helped to found other benevolent organizations such as the Society for the Relief of Poor Widows
with Small Children. It is not possible to calculate the value of the
benevolent work performed over the years by the churches, nor the
numbers of lives enhanced, healed, and made more whole by churches
living out the mandates of the gospel in the world.

Slavery presented the new republic and its churches with an enormous moral, political, and economic challenge. Estimates vary, but
between 3 and 5 million Africans were captured, transported across
the ocean in crowded, filthy slave ships—perhaps as many as half died
during the journey—and sold in auctions throughout the United
States. Neither the Constitution nor the Bill of Rights, with their high
philosophy of divinely inspired liberty, mention the tragic anomaly of
slavery, although Jefferson himself seems to have understood that the
elimination of the shameful institution would occupy his nation for
years to come.

The record of the churches is not heroic. In 1787, the Presbyterian
Synod of New York and Philadelphia issued a proclamation that all
human beings are created by God, condemned slavery, and urged its
gradual abolition. The General Assembly endorsed the condemnation
but over the years softened its position. In the South, some Presbyterians began to defend slavery as a biblical institution, but the abolition
movement would not be silenced. Other Presbyterians, including a
group of African American pastors, spoke out against the involuntary
enslavement of human beings. In St. Louis, an angry mob destroyed
the printing presses of Presbyterian minister Elijah Lovejoy. Lovejoy,
whose newspaper attacked the institution of slavery, was murdered by
another mob in Alton, Illinois, in 1837 and became a symbol of Presbyterian commitment to freedom for all God's children.

In 1861, southern Presbyterians withdrew from the General Assembly after a resolution offered by William C. Anderson mandated support of the Union. (William Anderson was the great-grandfather of
Harrison Ray Anderson, moderator of the 192nd General Assembly,
who worked tirelessly for the reunion of the separated Presbyterian
Church a century later.) On the topic of slavery, the southern church

acknowledged that slavery was the issue dividing the nation and lead-ing to war, but defended the institution on biblical and philosophic grounds. The Presbyterian Church in the Confederate States of Amer-ica was formed and existed as the Presbyterian Church in the United States until 1983, when the separated denominations reunited and became the Presbyterian Church (U.S.A.).

The churches also mostly missed the tragic anomaly of Native Americans who were treated as unwelcome aliens in their own land. The church's attention to the plight of Native Americans was mainly in evangelization, for the most part ignoring the question of justice. There were, of course, glorious exceptions. When the State of Geor-gia took Cherokee land and sent the Cherokee people on the Trail of Tears to Oklahoma, Presbyterian missionary Samuel Worcester protested, and then was arrested and sentenced to a Georgia prison. After his release, Worcester accompanied the Cherokee people on their tragic journey.

Westward growth characterized the early decades of the nineteenth century, and the churches followed the frontier over the mountains and into the western territories of Ohio and Kentucky. Presbyterians con-tinued to insist on university-trained and ordained pastors and were far less innovative and responsive to the new situation than the Meth-odists and Baptists, who recruited many missionaries, carrying a Bible on horseback to the frontier to plant new churches. The Presbyterian numerical superiority of Colonial days began to fall behind.

Ministers, missionaries, and circuit riders held preaching missions and revival meetings in frontier communities and sometimes in wilder-ness clearings. Pioneers traveled for miles to see and meet neighbors, enjoying a few days of fellowship and worship. A new church—Methodist, Baptist, sometimes Presbyterian—was often the result.

Back in the East, Presbyterians joined with Congregationalists and others in new missionary agencies to evangelize the frontier and also to obey Jesus' mandate to go into all the world and preach the gospel. Presbyterians and Congregationalists even approved a Plan of Union in 1801 designed to foster missionary cooperation. Presbyterians also joined other church leaders in 1810 to form the American Board of Commissioners for Foreign Mission.

Presbyterian missionaries were an important part of the late-nineteenth- and twentieth-century expansion of global mission. American Presbyterians sailed from East Coast and West Coast port cities to South and Central America, Cuba, Africa, China, Japan, and Korea. Thriving Reformed Presbyterian Churches in Brazil, Cuba, Kenya, Sudan, and Korea today play major roles in these nations, and many of them send missionaries into the world, sometimes to the United States. Portuguese-speaking Brazilian Presbyterian missionaries work in American inner cities. Sudanese pastors serve Sudanese refugee congregations in New York. Korean Presbyterian missionaries serve growing Presbyterian congregations in Santiago, Chile.

The Reverend Horace Underwood and his wife, Lilias Sterling Underwood, MD, went to Korea in 1885, among the first Protestant missionaries to arrive there. Roman Catholic missionaries had been in Korea for years, and there was an American Methodist on the same ship as the Underwoods; Presbyterians and Methodists thus share the honor of arriving early. The Underwoods went to work immediately with great energy and creativity: preaching, teaching, healing, and establishing churches and clinics.

Presbyterian missionaries traditionally have responded to the Great Commission of Jesus to "go therefore and make disciples of all nations" (Matt. 28:19), and also our Lord's Great Commandment to love neighbor as oneself by feeding the hungry, clothing the naked, and visiting the sick and imprisoned (Matt. 25:31–45).

The vitality of the church in Korea today stems from that balanced missionary emphasis—preaching good news and exhibiting love of neighbor. The churches that Horace Underwood planted in Korea have grown and matured and today extend into the world their evangelical love and passion for social justice. Dr. Lilias Sterling Underwood's gift of healing continues in great Christian medical and educational institutions, such as Severance Hospital in Seoul.

Shortly after the Underwoods arrived in Korea, the nation was stricken by a cholera epidemic. Isolation was the only treatment for infected and dying people who were, for the sake of the health of the rest of the family, often abandoned. Korean Christians amazed their neighbors by going into the streets to minister to dying neighbors, sometimes transporting them to Severance Hospital. So astonishing was this brave and compassionate behavior that the emperor sent to know who these angels were. When the emperor's wife fell ill, he sent for Lilias Sterling Underwood, whose medical skill and compassion assisted the empress's recovery. In gratitude, the emperor began to consult with Dr. Underwood, who subsequently advised the Korean government on health-care policy, sanitation, and hygiene. The Underwoods' story is repeated all over the world, wherever men and women, in the name of Jesus Christ and with the support of the church, proclaim the good news of God's love—and then express that love in acts of kindness, compassion, and justice.

Reformed Presbyterian commitment to education, rooted in the heritage of John Calvin and John Knox, resulted in the establishment of many colleges and universities, sometimes in cooperation with Congregationalists and others, and sometimes unilaterally. The College of Wooster in Ohio, Lafayette College in Pennsylvania, Hampden Sydney College in Virginia, Davidson College in North Carolina, Agnes Scott College, Macalester College, Rhodes College, Milliken University, and the University of Tulsa were all founded by Presbyterians and the Presbyterian Church. Sixty-eight of those colleges are still related to the General Assembly of the Presbyterian Church (U.S.A.).

Equally important, Presbyterians worked for the establishment of state-supported public universities, open to all people. Some of these include the Universities of Michigan, Ohio, North Carolina, Tennessee, and California. Presbyterians established colleges for women and, after the Civil War, more than one hundred elementary and secondary schools, junior colleges, and colleges for children of emancipated slaves. A number of these distinguished institutions continue to serve primarily African American student bodies: Knoxville, Mary Holmes, Barber-Scotia, Tusculum, and Stillman.

As the nation spread across the continent to the Pacific Ocean, Presbyterians followed and built churches. Presbyterian physician Marcus Whitman and the Reverend Henry S. Spaulding organized churches and clinics for Native Americans along the Oregon Trail in 1834. Narcissa Whitman and Eliza Spaulding were the first European American women to make the journey. The Whitmans were subsequently killed by Native Americans who believed they had caused a measles epidemic.

Sheldon Jackson preached and organized Presbyterian churches in Wyoming, Montana, Idaho, Utah, and Alaska. Presbyterian missionaries not only went to China and Africa, but on the West Coast, Presbyterian settlement houses served the arriving populations from the Far East. John Calvin insisted that the Christian religion was expressed in the life of the city of Geneva, its laws and jurisprudence, its market practices and educational policies. John Knox argued for universal education provided by state taxation. Both met considerable opposition from people who argued that religion ought not be confused with politics or economics, and the church ought not to meddle in the political, economic, and social life of society. The heirs of Calvin and Knox followed their example from the beginning by extending the influence of their Presbyterian church into the life of the society.

In the nineteenth century, Presbyterians vigorously advocated for Sabbath observance, not only by church people, but by society at large. Their point was that Sabbath observance is a way of testifying to God's sovereignty over all of life, and that all citizens, even nonbelievers, would benefit from a day of rest. Over the years, American society has gradually eliminated any sense of a Sabbath while new information technology assures that market activity continues twenty-four hours a day, seven days a week. Suddenly the old Presbyterian notion of an enforced Sabbath sounds like a good, life-giving, healthy idea!

From the beginning, Presbyterians have assumed responsibility for the life of society whether the society welcomes or wants Presbyterian responsibility or not. Presbyterians have opinions on everything. Not all supported Prohibition, but Presbyterians for a century had been arguing for temperance and moderation in the use of alcoholic beverages. As early as 1828, Presbyterians were advocating and organizing for peace and pacifism as an alternative to the tragedy and waste of war.

As the churches confronted the twentieth century, none could anticipate the challenges that lay immediately ahead: the rise of totalitarianism, global war, the urgent cause of human rights (including the emerging role of women), ecumenism, and a dramatic shift in the position of the old mainline churches in American and global culture.

Is the church viable, or in God's economy, has the institutional church run its course? Does the continuing numerical attrition signal the ultimate demise of the institution as we know it, or is God up to something new and exciting—something that will emerge from within the church?

To the modern church, the church of the twentieth and twenty-first centuries, the future of the church, we now turn our attention.

7

The Church as Living Reminder

*T*he earliest church was called into existence by the presence of the risen Christ. It was a visible reminder to the world that Jesus had lived and taught and healed: that he lived in Galilee, traveled to Jerusalem where he was crucified, and that after his death on the cross, his disciples experienced him in their midst. A few years later, Paul would create an unforgettable metaphor to describe the church—"the body of Christ"—the living reminder of who he was and is.

Someone once described the mission of the modern urban church as "keeping alive the rumor that there is a God." That is what the church of the future must do and be—a living reminder of Jesus, God's incarnate Son: a reminder to a busy, secular, preoccupied world of the transcendent, the holy, and the sacred in the midst of life.

Church buildings themselves—sometimes elegant, sometimes ordinary, sometimes beautiful, sometimes ugly—are nevertheless reminders of the presence of God in the life of the world.

Author Kathleen Norris, a Presbyterian, describes her church in South Dakota:

> Hope Church is an unassuming frame building that stands in a pasture at the edge of a coulee where ash trees and berry bushes flourish. . . . The place doesn't look like much, even when most of the membership has arrived on Sunday morning, yet it's one of the most successful churches I know. . . . Hope Church gives the people who live around it a sense of identity.[1]

What transpires inside church buildings is counterculture activity in the world of the future, activity with no market value and little entertainment potential. It is called worship—the intentional bringing of life into God's presence, the corporate offering of gratitude and praise to the Creator and giver of life, the communal listening for a word from the Lord and a renewal of commitment to live in the world as God's people.

One of the pacesetters and most successful business leaders in the information technology economy that characterizes our culture, a man to whom many look for words of wisdom, was asked if he goes to church on Sunday morning. His answer was significant. He said, "Just in terms of the use of time, going to church isn't very efficient."[2] Exactly. But when people gather to worship they are expressing something that is a permanent part of the human story, something that is a part of what it means to be human, something Augustine of Hippo meant when he wrote, "Thou hast made our hearts restless until they find their rest in Thee." Worship is the primal human activity to which we are invited by the psalmist.

> O come, let us worship and bow down,
>   let us kneel before the LORD, our Maker!
> For he is our God,
>   and we are the people of his pasture,
>   and the sheep of his hand.
>   (Ps. 95:6–7)

The church of the future will grapple with issues of style and strategy, whether music ought to be four hundred years old and played on a pipe organ or composed last week in a Nashville studio and accompanied by electric guitars and drums. Musicians and theologians will debate and argue, and someone will repeat what Martin Luther reportedly asked when criticized for using German drinking songs as hymns: "Why should the devil have all the good tunes?"

It will be a mixed future, stylistically, as it should be, with some churches expressing the best of our past and other churches experimenting with new forms and new music and a new aesthetic for a new age. But beyond questions of style—robes or business attire, hymnals or pull-down screens, organ or praise band—the worship of the church will give the world a desperately needed gift: a reminder of the presence of the living God in the life of the world.

Body of Christ

When the church gathers to worship it reminds the world that there is a God, a holy transcendent One, and that God has come to be a part of human history in the life, death, and resurrection of Jesus Christ, and furthermore that God calls a people to live in and serve the world God so dearly loves. It is the glory and the great challenge of the church that God means for it to be an instrument of God's saving love for the world. When he understood the lofty nature and mission of the church that he helped to establish, Paul said the most astonishing thing about it: "Now you are the body of Christ and individually members of it" (1 Cor. 12:27). Think of it! Those modest little communities gathering secretly in one another's homes to break bread and drink wine two thousand years ago and your church, the congregation that gathers to worship, witness, and serve, at First Presbyterian, Trinity Lutheran, Holy Name Cathedral—the body of Christ!

Paul understood that when people become church there is something more happening than the normal human search for God. Human beings have always pondered the mystery of life, how we got here, and what life is for. We are "God obsessed," as the theologians sometimes put it. When people become church, Paul suggests, God is doing something, taking the initiative, calling, forming, inspiring, and equipping people to be a new reality—Christ's body on earth.

Thus, while the church is a reminder to the world, it is also, we believe, the way God continues to be in and to love and to save the world. The church is, we believe, part of the incarnational love of God that was given in Jesus Christ. The church is his body, which continues to be present in the world.

There are reminders for the church of its identity and mission. They are called sacraments. They are actions that occurred in the life of Jesus himself: baptism and the Lord's Supper. The sacraments of the church are described in various ways. Sacraments are "outward signs of an inner truth." Baptism and Communion are visible signs or symbols of God's love in Jesus Christ. Sacraments are simple acts that contain deep and wonderful mystery. Sacraments are a means of grace, ways by which God conveys to us, and we experience as individuals, a reality that mere words cannot contain. We know how difficult it is, sometimes impossible, to put into words our deepest, most profound feelings. Saying "I love you" to our dearest beloved, our children, and our spouses sometimes simply is not adequate. And so we give a gift, flowers, a ring, a sometimes simple, sometimes extravagant symbol of what we want to say. There is something like that in the sacraments of the church.

Baptism

At one time or another, many of us were carried into a church by our proud parents for our baptism. It was a big day for them and for us. They dressed us especially for the occasion, in a gown others wore before us for their baptism, or new clothes purchased for this day. They invited others to be present: grandparents, aunts and uncles, close friends. They may even have invited everyone back to our home for lunch to continue the celebration.

Three promises were made that day. When our parents walked to the front of the church and presented us to the minister, they were asked to reaffirm their own faith in Jesus Christ and they promised to share that faith in Jesus Christ, to share that faith with us as we grew into childhood, adolescence, and adulthood. The minister also asked the congregation sitting in the pews that Sunday if they would assume some responsibilities in the project of conveying Christian faith to us. "Will you, the people of the church, promise to tell this new disciple the good news of the gospel, to help him/her know all that Christ commands, and, by your fellowship, to strengthen his/her family ties with the household of God?" The people of the congregation promised that day, and they made good on their promise. They provided Christian education and youth activities and a community to which we belonged. And when the minister had prayed and placed water from the baptismal font on our head, he or she made another promise. In these words or words similar the minister said, "Rachel, Cameron, Katherine, John, you are a child of the covenant, sealed by the Spirit. You belong to Jesus Christ forever." That is quite a promise. In our baptism we are attached to and belong to Jesus Christ for the rest of our lives and beyond.

No minister presides at the sacrament of baptism without experiencing a sense of God's steadfast and unconditional love. No parent watches as the water of baptism is gently touched to their infant's brow without experiencing the indescribable grace of God. No congregation witnesses baptism and promises to love and care for this newest member of the community without knowing the mysterious reality of the church as the body of Christ.

Some are baptized later, during adolescence, when Christian faith is claimed personally. Some are baptized as adults, kneeling in front of the congregation, or immersed in water, while the minister says those same words: "I baptize you in the name of the Father and the Son and the Holy Spirit. You belong to Jesus Christ forever."

Baptism is a reminder of the mystery of God's love in Jesus Christ. It also takes us into deep water theologically. Jesus was baptized in the Jordan River by his cousin John the Baptist. For him it was the occasion when he knew himself to be God's beloved Son, and it was the beginning of his life of obedient faithfulness to his public ministry. Later, Paul would say that in baptism we participate in Jesus' death and resurrection, that as the water of baptism flows over us we die to sin and everything that separates us from God and rise again to our new lives as children of God. We spend the rest of our lives living out the mystery of our baptism (see Rom. 6:1–11).

The water of baptism reminds us of the waters of creation, the waters of the flood, the waters of the Red Sea through which God's people miraculously walked in the exodus. The water of baptism reminds us of the goodness of God's creation and God's covenant promise. It reminds us of God's new covenant with humankind and with us, in Jesus Christ.

And baptism reminds us of the universal reality of the church. In baptism we remember that by the Holy Spirit, we are mystically linked with the church in every time and place.

On a bright sunny day, beneath a brilliantly blue Mediterranean sky, five American Presbyterians were walking up a steep winding street on the Greek island of Santorini. They heard singing, the distinct sound of a religious chant. Following the sound of the music they stepped inside a small Greek Orthodox church. A crowd of twenty-five or thirty people of all ages gathered in the front, an Orthodox priest presiding. It was a baptism. The Americans started to leave as inconspicuously as possible, but one of the worshipers noticed and gestured for them to stay, to come closer, to see better. A baby was handed to the priest, who removed him from his blanket, held him up for all to see, naked, plunged him into the font, held him up again for all to see, blubbering, dripping wet, now squawling over the shock of what had just happened. His family was pleased, murmuring, oohing, and ahhing. The service continued to its end. Again the Americans began to leave and again were motioned to remain. It wasn't over yet. An elderly woman began to distribute small medallions of an infant boy's head fastened to a blue ribbon with a pin to attach to clothing. Everyone did it, the grateful American Presbyterians included. They had been part of a baptism; they were now, by the power of God's Holy Spirit, part of the newly baptized baby's family of faith, the body of Christ.

A delegation of American Christians were visiting a congregation in Cuba, the First Presbyterian Church of Havana. On Sunday morning during worship, a baptism was scheduled. The Cuban pastor invited his American counterpart to participate, which he gratefully did, saying the words, "Anibal, I baptize you . . ." in English after the Cuban pastor's Spanish. It was a powerful experience for all those present, Cuban and American Christians, of the way baptism overcomes barriers of nationality, history, language, politics, all the barriers that separate the human race. When the Americans returned home they put a rosebud in the church, which they normally do to celebrate a birth in the congregation. This rosebud, however, celebrated the baptism of Anibal Quesada, who in her baptism belongs to Jesus Christ forever, and is part of the great family of God's people, everywhere, the body of Christ.

The Church as Beloved Community

*T*he gift of the Spirit to the gathered Christians at Pentecost was communication; each could hear and understand, and people spoke to and listened to one another. Communication—Communion—community—God's good gifts to the church and the churches' gifts to give to the world.

The church of the future will be effective and relevant to the degree that it understands itself as a beloved community. The degree to which it does not look like and behave like a beloved community is the degree to which the world will dismiss the church as irrelevant.

Why is it that the church has found it so very difficult to be the beloved community of God's people? Novelist Mary McCarthy once quipped that "religion makes good people good and bad people bad."[1] Jonathan Swift observed, "We have just enough religion to make us hate one another, but not enough to make us love one another."[2]

The everlasting shame of the church is that Christians reserve a particular meanness and hostility for each other. During the dreadful violence in Central Europe, Serbian nationalists blew up the Roman Catholic cathedral in the Croatian town of Vinkovci. Croatian Catholic nationalists retaliated by blowing up the Orthodox cathedral. Evangelical Christians target Roman Catholic Christians, and when their efforts are successful they call it "conversion." Southern Baptists refuse to sit down with other Baptists, and Missouri Synod Lutherans decline to participate in ecumenical worship services. The Vatican releases a theological statement that declares that the Roman Catholic Church

/ 63

is the only agent of salvation. And some Presbyterians create a list of irreconcilable differences with other Presbyterians and invite them to leave, offering to hold the back door open for their convenient departure. Others try to superimpose their own theologies and ideologies onto the church, claiming that their particular interpretation of specific doctrines represents the absolute truth and the orthodoxy to which the church has always subscribed.

It is not a new story. Around AD 55, in the Greek port city of Corinth, the tiny Christian church was making a public spectacle of itself because of its internal divisions and public conflicts. Paul's letter to that early church sounds as if it might have been written today and addressed to American Presbyterians, Methodists, or Lutherans: "Now I appeal to you, brothers and sisters, by the name of our Lord Jesus Christ, that all of you be in agreement and that there be no divisions among you, but that you be united in the same mind and the same purpose. . . . Has Christ been divided?" (1 Cor. 1:10, 13). Christian disunity is an embarrassment to Christ and renders the church irrelevant to the world. On the very night of his betrayal and arrest, Jesus prayed for his disciples "that they may all be one. As you, Father, are in me and I am in you, may they also be in us, so that the world may believe that you have sent me" (John 17:21).

There is an evangelical imperative for the unity of the church. The world can see something of the reality of God and the truth of Jesus Christ in the quality of human relationships that characterize the church. Or, to put it the other way, the world simply isn't interested in our internal divisions and is bored by our incessant arguing.

The world needs the gift of community. The world needs a reminder that each life, each person, is precious, a beloved child of God deserving of respect, care, justice, and compassion. The world needs to see what a community looks like, needs a place to go to satisfy the hunger for community. Jesus himself described the human condition more in terms of lostness than sinfulness (Luke 15; John 10), and his most beloved story was about a prodigal's homecoming reunion with family and community (Luke 15).

The church is most thoroughly the church when it becomes a beloved community, and it is most effective as a proclamation of good news when it extends the hospitality of Jesus Christ to the stranger, the lonely, the lost, and the outcast. Community is a gift of the Spirit to be received in gratitude. It begins in the heart of the believer who knows herself/himself to be the recipient of God's welcome and hospitality. Sometimes community happens in the church in spite of us.

A freshly minted pastor in a small rural church confidently announces that the annual women's bazaar and men's spaghetti dinner are inappropriate because they market religion, turn a handsome profit for their respective organizations, undermine good stewardship practices, and transform the gospel of Jesus Christ into a product, a pot-scratcher, or plate of spaghetti and meatballs. The presidents of the women's association and men's fellowship are equally dismayed to be told by their new pastor that their favorite activities are inappropriate. "But they raise money for the Lord's work," they explain, and add, "Besides, we have a lot of fun together." The new pastor is bright enough not to insist on his own way and, instead of terminating the bazaar/spaghetti dinner by ministerial fiat, actually accepts the invitation to attend and participate. He works at the bazaar book stall, watching and listening as people talk and share common joys and concerns and touch each other with love and mutuality. Elbow deep in the pot of spaghetti sauce, he watches and listens as men banter and joke and laugh and tentatively share their hopes and fears. The new minister, in spite of what he has learned about church stewardship, discovers the gift of community; he concludes that while it may not be Pentecost, it is no less a miracle of God's grace.

Much of the New Testament following the four Gospels is devoted to the subject of the life, in community, of the early Christian church. In his letters to those churches Paul comments on the status of the community: "Now I appeal to you, brothers and sisters, . . . be united in the same mind" (1 Cor. 1:10); scolds the believers for the failure of community: "For as long as there is jealousy and quarreling among you, are you not of the flesh, and behaving according to human inclinations?" (1 Cor. 3:3); admonishes them to live in community with one another: "I therefore, the prisoner in the Lord, beg you to lead a life worthy of the calling to which you have been called, with all humility and gentleness, with patience, bearing with one another in love, making every effort to maintain the unity of the Spirit in the bond of peace" (Eph. 4:1–4); and urges them to live in community: "As

God's chosen ones, holy and beloved, clothe yourselves with compassion, kindness, humility, meekness, and patience. Bear with one another and, if anyone has a complaint against another, forgive each other; just as the Lord has forgiven you. . . . Above all, clothe yourselves with love, which binds everything together in perfect harmony" (Col. 3:12–14).

Paul's vision of the church as the beloved community is a major New Testament theme, expressed nowhere more eloquently than the letter to the church at Colossae: "Let the peace of Christ rule in your hearts, to which indeed you were called in the one body. . . . And whatever you do, in word or deed, do everything in the name of the Lord Jesus, giving thanks to God the Father through him" (Col. 3:15, 17).

Life in the new community of Christ, the church, is central to Paul's thinking, both his ecclesiology and theology. In thousands of churches every Saturday afternoon, during the celebration of marriage, the minister reads, at the couple's request, the thirteenth chapter of Paul's First Letter to the Corinthians. It is one of the most beloved and familiar passages of Scripture, but is is not about marriage at all. It is part, the key part, of Paul's admonition to the members of the church at Corinth to stop arguing, fighting, and name-calling, and to start acting like Christians, members of the beloved community, the body of Christ: "And I will show you a still more excellent way. . . . If I speak in the tongues of mortals and angels, but do not have love, I am a noisy gong or clanging cymbal. . . . Love never ends. . . . And now faith, hope, and love abide, these three; and the greatest of these is love" (1 Cor. 12:31; 13:1, 8, 13). For Paul, the very heart of the Christian enterprise is the new community of Christ, which shows the world by the way it lives, its visible humility, forgiveness, and love, the very love of God revealed in Jesus Christ.

At one of the most critical and threatening moments in our history, the rise of Nazism in Germany in the 1930s, a young theologian realized that the Christian community was the reality, the force that could and must confront fascist totalitarianism. The German church, in many ways like the current American church, had become radically individualistic. Religion was a matter of the individual's feelings, emotion, and spirit. Although the word was not yet in use, German religion and piety in the 1930s could be described as "spirituality."

Dietrich Bonhoeffer understood that the integrity and survival of the church in Germany depended on a renewal of the community nature of the church. In addition to the twentieth-century classic *The Cost of Discipleship*, Bonhoeffer wrote about the strength and power and absolute importance of community in *Life Together*. It is a small book that tells about the discipline of community among the students at a seminary Bonhoeffer established at Finkenwald. He understood that clergy and churches strong enough to resist Hitler would depend on a "revitalization of discipleship learned and lived in Christian community for the sake of service in and to the world."[3] The Nazis understood too. They shut down Finkenwald in 1937, drafted most of the students into military service, and on April 9, 1945, executed Bonhoeffer as a traitor.

The church's vision of itself as a community of individuals bound to one another by the love, forgiveness, judgment, and grace of Jesus Christ is fundamental to its life in the world and its future. The visible symbol and agent of that beloved community is the sacrament of the Lord's Supper, Communion.

> For I received from the Lord what I also handed on to you, that the Lord Jesus on the night when he was betrayed took a loaf of bread, and when he had given thanks, he broke it and said, "This is my body that is for you. Do this in remembrance of me." In the same way he took the cup also, after supper, saying, "This cup is the new covenant in my blood. Do this, as often as you drink it, in remembrance of me." For as often as you eat this bread and drink the cup, you proclaim the Lord's death until he comes. (1 Cor. 11:23–26)

That is how Paul instructed the church at Corinth to observe, or "practice," the act of remembering Jesus, as they gathered for weekly worship. All four Gospels tell us that on the night of his arrest, the Thursday of the last week of his earthly life, Jesus invited his disciples to a meal. His instruction to them about the place and the preparation were precise. It was not yet the Passover, but it may have been a pre-Passover meal in light of his own sense of the plot to arrest him. The Gospel of John tells us that before they ate, Jesus washed their feet. And then, all four accounts agree, he did something none of them, or none of us, have been able to forget. He broke the bread and told them it was his body, broken for them. He gave thanks and passed a cup of wine among them and told them it was his blood, shed for them. He told them all—Peter who was about to deny him, Judas who would betray him, Thomas who doubted him, all of them—to drink from one cup.

And so, ever since, his followers, his church, have been saying the words, eating the bread, and drinking the wine in remembrance of him. Different churches interpret and practice the sacrament differently and call it by different names: Eucharist, from the Greek word for "thanksgiving," Holy Communion, the Lord's Supper. It is the high point of the Roman Catholic mass when, according to Catholic doctrine, the bread and wine are transformed into the actual body and blood of Christ. It is the central act of worship for Episcopalians, Lutherans, and Methodists. In those traditions, as well as Roman Catholicism, worshipers approach the chancel, or front of the church, and either kneel or stand to receive the elements from the clergy. In Presbyterian and Reformed churches, worshipers are served the elements by elders and deacons, and the people often pass the elements, literally serving one another.

All Christian churches, despite differences in theology and practice, believe that Jesus Christ is mysteriously present in the sacrament, that God's mercy, grace, forgiveness, and love are available to us in the bread broken and cup poured, and that the regular observance of the sacrament is both a sign and concrete evidence of the beloved community of the church. Christians also believe that the sacrament is a promise that Christ's redeeming work in the world will continue in the future until all is complete, and he comes again.

The sacrament of the Lord's Supper is also an act of thanksgiving (Eucharist) for God's goodness that we see in creation, in the history of God's people down through the centuries, and particularly in the gift of Jesus Christ. The elements of bread and wine, or grape juice, represent for us the bounty of God's creation that sustains us. The act of eating together also reminds us of Christ's presence in all of life and of the sanctity and blessedness of every meal we eat.

The specific practices of Communion vary:

- In a cathedral mass, with Gregorian chant, incense, and elaborate liturgy.

- In an African village around a simple wooden table beneath a tent.
- In a highland kirk where the small communion shelf on the back of each pew is lovingly covered with a white linen cloth.
- By the bedside of a critically ill patient facing the final mystery.
- On a battlefield where young men and women face the valley of the shadow.
- In your local congregation, when you sit in your pew and receive the bread and cup from a neighbor on your left and serve them to the stranger on your right.

The sacrament of the Lord's Supper is the way the beloved community remembers its Lord, and the way God chooses to convey the love and grace and holy presence of Jesus Christ to us.

Communion always reminds us of those who have preceded us, our dear ones who come to the Table before us, and all the faithful in all times and places who are bound together by Christ's love. We call it the Communion of Saints.

It is Christ's Table. As we gather around it we remember how he welcomed all who would come, how he extended hospitality to those who were excluded and marginalized in his time. As we eat and drink with our neighbors and with him, we remember how he was criticized for eating and drinking with sinners. Some churches restrict access to the sacrament to their own members. In the Presbyterian tradition the Invitation to the Table is made to any and all who trust in Jesus Christ. Ours is an open communion, and we work and pray for the day when the scandal of the church's brokenness will be healed and all will be welcome at Christ's Table.

In the Church of Scotland the minister sometimes invites worshipers to the sacrament of the Lord's Supper with these words:

> Come to the table not because you are strong,
> but because you understand something of your own weakness.
> Come to the table not because you feel worthy,
> but because you have a sense of your own unworthiness;
> come not because you love God a lot,
> but because you love God a little
> and want to learn to love God more.[4]

The Beloved Community as Home

Writer Anne Lamott, who returned to Christian faith and the church in response to the irresistible power of an authentic Christian community, describes her new congregation in warmly affectionate terms. Lamott passes on a story her pastor, Veronica, told.

> A tall African-American woman named Veronica came to lead us. She has huge gentle doctor hands, with dimples where the knuckles should be, like a baby's fists. She stepped into us, the wonderful old worn pair of pants that is St. Andrew, and they fit. She sings to us sometimes from the pulpit and tells us stories of when she was a child. She told us this story just the other day. When she was about seven, her best friend got lost one day. The little girl ran up and down the streets of the big town where they lived, but she couldn't find a single landmark. She was very frightened. Finally a policeman stopped to help her. He put her in the passenger seat of his car, and they drove around until she finally saw church. She pointed it out to the policeman, and then she told him firmly, "You could let me out now. This is my church, and I can always find my way home from here."
>
> And that is why I have stayed so close to mine—because no matter how bad I am feeling, how lost or lonely or frightened, when I see the faces of the people at my church, and hear their tawny voices, I can always find my way home.[5]

A pastor was visiting a young man with HIV-AIDS in a hospice facility. Glen's childhood church had let him and his family know that because of his sexual orientation and practice, he was not welcome. And so he sought refuge in a large urban congregation that was more inclusive. He was in worship every Sunday and participated in as many of the congregation's outreach ministries as his declining health would allow. Now he was dying. At the end of a good conversation about life and death, fear and hope and resurrection, I asked, "What is the hardest part of this, Glen?"

Glen answered, "It's at the end of the day, when the guests are all gone and it's quiet and they turn the lights out and I'm alone with my thoughts and my fears." Glen smiled and continued, "Do you know

what I do then? I get out my tape player and listen to a worship service at our church. I listen to the whole thing, the hymns, the prayers,
the announcements. Sometimes I fall asleep during your sermon," he
added with a twinkle in his eye. "That's how I fall to sleep every night.
Here in my bed. But also in my church."

The world needs to know what a beloved community looks like.
God means to give the world that gift. God's gift is the church.

9

A Sign of the Kingdom

The great ends of the church are the proclamation of the gospel for the salvation of humankind; the shelter, nurture, and spiritual fellowship of the children of God; the maintenance of divine worship; the preservation of the truth; the promotion of social righteousness; and the exhibition of the Kingdom of Heaven to the world.[1]

A provisional exhibition/demonstration of the reign of God. It has been about transformation from the beginning, the transformation of the individual by the grace, forgiveness, and love of God in Jesus Christ, and the transformation of the world into God's intent, God's kingdom, God's commonwealth. At Mount Sinai, the people of God were given ten laws that regulated their relationship with God and also the way they lived together in society—economically, politically, personally.

From the very beginning the story of God's people is the story of a people with a mission. God calls Abram and Sara to pick up and move from their traditional home in Haran, where they had lived for years, accumulating wealth and becoming comfortable, to strike out on a new journey. They are to go to a new place and begin a new adventure. And they have an assignment: they are to be a blessing. God tells Abram, "I will make of you a great nation, and I will bless you, and make your name great, so that you will be a blessing" (Gen. 12:2).

Israel is to live in the world in a way that the world will see something of the love and justice of God. Israel's chosenness is not for its own edification and pleasure. It is for the world.

I am the LORD, I have called you in righteousness,
   I have taken you by the hand and kept you;
I have given you as a covenant to the people,
   a light to the nations,
     to open the eyes that are blind,
   to bring out the prisoners from the dungeon,
     from the prison those who sit in darkness.
                           (Isa. 42:6–7)

Israel is called to a vocation that takes it out of itself and into the world. God's people have a job to do in the world: "to be a light to the nations."

Jewish theologian Irving Greenberg urges Christians and Jews to acknowledge their covenant partnership with each other and with God for the purpose of repairing and healing the world (Tikun Olam).[2] The mission of God's people is to live in the world in a way that visibly demonstrates the values and truth of God's reign, and to work with God to bring about that reign on earth. That means that God's people will always live intentionally in the world and become involved in the world; the church will always find itself enmeshed in worldly matters—politics, economics, the way the poor and imprisoned are treated, the sick cared for, children educated—not to advance a particular political agenda, but because God calls God's people, in every age, to mission in the world.

Biblical scholars help us understand that the uniqueness of the story of God and God's people is precisely that it is about theology and sociology, a way of believing in God and a way of living with one's neighbors. Believing in God puts one into a new social contract. The weakest of the weak, orphans and widows—struggling to survive in a patriarchal culture—are to receive special attention. So is the alien, the stranger, the poor. In fact, to guarantee that economics will not determine the social contract as it does in every other nation, in ancient Israel debt will not extend more than six years, and every fifty years, at the Jubilee, all accounts are declared paid in full and everybody returns to equal status. Some historians doubt that Jubilee was ever actually enacted. And yet it is a remarkable idea. It is a remarkable arrangement, and its purpose is to honor God's oneness and holiness and also the neighbor's dignity, autonomy, and freedom. Walter Brueggemann observes that in this tradition, "You cannot say 'God' without saying 'neighbor.' In the Bible it becomes a new, hyphenated name: 'God-neighbor.'" [3]

It is a defining moment when Jesus is asked, "Which commandment is the first of all," and he answers with two: "'You shall love the Lord your God with all your heart, and with all your soul, and with all your mind, and with all your strength.' The second is this, 'You shall love your neighbor as yourself'" (Mark 12:29–31).

It is both/and, and not either/or; God and neighbor, theology and mission, personal transformation and social transformation, evangelism and social action.

After he had called his disciples and instructed them about the values and practices of God's kingdom, Jesus sent them out into the towns and countryside of Galilee to go to work. He told them to "proclaim the good news, 'The kingdom of heaven has come near.' Cure the sick, raise the dead, cleanse the lepers, cast out demons" (Matt. 10:5–10). Jesus wants his followers to know that God has work for them to do similar to God's ancient summons to Israel to be a "light to the nations," proclaiming, witnessing, healing, cleansing, shining the light of God's love into all the world and into every place and incident of darkness.

At the very end of the story of his life the risen Christ meets his friends in the early light of dawn, on the beach. They were in a boat, fishing. After the tumultuous, frightening, and mysterious events of his betrayal, arrest, crucifixion, and the experience of his resurrection, his disciples have returned to the safety and security of the familiar. They see Jesus standing on the beach. He invites them to join him for breakfast. He has prepared a fire, with fish and bread.

Jesus feeds them and then initiates a dialogue with Simon Peter, who had denied even knowing Jesus several days before: "'Simon son of John, do you love me more than these?' . . . 'Yes, Lord; you know that I love you.' Jesus said to him, 'Feed my lambs'" (John 21:15). Peter had been questioned, accused of being a follower of Jesus three times in the dark courtyard on the night of his arrest. Three times Peter, to save himself from arrest and perhaps crucifixion, denied that he knew Jesus. So now the question comes three times, "Do you love me?" Three times Peter affirms his love for Jesus, and three times the charge is repeated: "Feed my lambs. . . . Tend my sheep. . . . Feed my sheep" (John 21:15–17).

To love Jesus, to trust him and claim him as Lord and Savior, is to receive a commission, a vocation, a task to do. It is in the world. From the beginning to the end of the story, God's people are sent into the world with work to do: proclaiming, shining light, healing, cleansing, feeding and tending the sheep.

A generation after Jesus, an evangelist put it plainly and uncompromisingly:

> Those who say, "I love God," and hate their brothers and sisters, are liars; for those who do not love a brother or sister whom they have seen, cannot love God whom they have not seen. The commandment we have from him is this: those who love God must love their brothers and sisters also. (1 John 4:20–21)

So the church is called and commissioned by God to tell the good news of Jesus Christ and to show the good news in transformed relationships within and acts of love and justice in the world. The world is hungry for that kind of religious wholeness. There is plenty of evidence that modern men and women are not much interested in a religion that is entirely private and personal and has nothing to do with the world. There is also evidence that modern men and women are not much compelled by church social service or social activist programs that are not related clearly and openly to belief in God and faith in Jesus Christ. There is plenty of evidence that when both occur in the life of a church, the gospel is communicated, Jesus Christ becomes real, and transformation, personal and social, begins to happen.

Studies of growing congregations, at a time when mainline denominations are declining numerically, consistently discover that the one characteristic that growing congregations share is not theology, ideology, or worship styles, but a sense of mission. Growing congregations are focused on the world outside the walls of their buildings and are intentional about translating the theological affirmations they make inside into acts of compassion, love, and justice outside. When institutional survival absorbs a church's energy and imagination and resources, it simply ceases to be very interesting or compelling. When a congregation lives out its faith in and for the sake of its Lord, it is difficult to ignore.

A tutoring program in a large metropolitan church serves four hundred children from a nearby public housing project plagued by violence, unemployment, and poverty. The tutors are all volunteers, mostly young urban adults working in law firms, banks, brokerage firms, and hospitals, mostly nonchurch members, and many nonbelievers or ex-believers. The tutors meet their young students once a week for an hour and a half in the church building. The church itself is growing, and in every monthly new members class there are always several young adults who make their witness:

> I was invited to be a tutor by a friend, signed up, worked with a student—in the church for six months. I began to care a lot about my student, and then one evening, I'm not sure why—maybe it was the music I heard from the choir rehearsal, or the picture of Jesus on the classroom wall, whatever—one evening I connected my being here tutoring a child with Jesus and what he said and stood for. So I started to attend on Sunday morning.

It is a powerful moment when the ministers of that church administer the sacrament of baptism to several young adults, kneeling in front of the congregation, often with tears of gratitude and love in their eyes.

Religion that expresses its theology in mission will communicate much about itself. Churches that hold together their beliefs about God and their love for the world and their neighbor will be vital churches.

The great temptation of the church has always been to turn away from the world. Partly it has been a matter of forgetting our identity and basic theological roots. Israel was called to be a "blessing to the nations, a light to the Gentiles." The identity and life of God's people was in the world. When the people became too preoccupied with themselves, when they forgot God's agenda and hopes, their prophets called them back:

> With what shall I come before the LORD, . . .
> Shall I come before him with burnt offerings. . . . ?
> Will the LORD be pleased with thousands of rams,
>   with ten thousands of rivers of oil? . . .

> He has told you, O mortal, what is good;
>   and what does the LORD require of you
> but to do justice, and to love kindness,
>   and to walk humbly with your God?
>   (Mic. 6:6–8, excerpts)

The central Christian affirmation is the incarnation. Christians believe that in Jesus Christ, God lived, was "enfleshed," which is what "incarnation" means. Countless volumes have been written in the differing and diverse attempts to understand and explain incarnation. What all believers agree is that when God came among us in Jesus Christ, it was an expression of God's love for the world. "For God so loved the world that he gave his only Son, so that everyone who believes in him may not perish but may have eternal life" (John 3:16). We are so familiar with that beloved text that we fail to recognize its radical and revolutionary content. God loves the world, this world, the world in which you and I were born and live out our lives. That is truly good news. It is still news because sometimes it seems like our religion concludes that the world is not worthy of God's love. In the past, forgetting our Hebrew roots and listening to the dualistic philosophy of Hellenism, Christianity has sometimes sounded as if it does not love this world at all, but instead calls people to live spiritual lives, separated from all that is worldly, bodily, including our basic, God-given humanity, human appetites, passion, hopes, and longings.

But it is this world that God so loves. And it is into this world that God calls the church to live and love and serve and give its life away.

Christian mission in the world happens in an astonishing array of activities, organized, funded, and carried out to express God's love in Jesus Christ. Churches, schools, colleges and universities, hospitals, clinics, nursing and medical schools, agricultural training and assistance, clean water and sanitation enhancement, family planning, small business development, affordable housing, seminaries and graduate schools of theology—it is impossible to travel anywhere in the world and not witness the way the church of Jesus Christ has expressed the love of God and the presence of God's reign.

During the terrible violence in Central Europe in the 1990s between ethnic groups in former Yugoslavia, Orthodox Serbians,

Croatians, Catholics, and Bosnian Muslims were caught in a devastating cycle of violence, retaliation, revenge, and death. In the middle of it all an ecumenical Protestant mission initiative attempted to show the presence of God's reign. A Serbian businessman, Antol Bolag, decided to dedicate his life to the promise of God's peace even in the midst of the ghastly ethnic cleansing and interfaith violence. He brought his business skills to a mission effort to rebuild and resettle Muslim families in villages destroyed in the war. Antol's job was to assemble the raw materials and labor, some paid and some volunteer, to rebuild Muslim villages, a house at a time. Reviewing reconstruction plans with the village chief, Antol was asked why his rebuilding plans included the reconstruction of the Muslim mosque.

"Why would you rebuild our mosque?" the Muslim chief asked Antol. "You Christians have been trying to convert us or kill us for centuries."

Antol answered: "We will rebuild your mosque because we follow One who commanded us to love our neighbors as ourselves; one who knelt by the side of the road to minister to a wounded brother without asking him about his theology."[4]

Every individual Christian, every denomination, every congregation is called to worldly mission. Even the smallest community of Christians has a vocation and can do something to express the radical good news that God loves this world enough to come among it in the life of his Son and to continue the work of redeeming, healing, and saving through his risen presence and the power of God's Spirit.

The world is watching and waiting. The world is seeking meaning and truth and hope in unprecedented ways at the beginning of the twenty-first century. And the church knows a secret that was given to it two thousand years ago. What the world wants and seeks and needs is the good news of God's love revealed in the one who said, "Those who want to save their life will lose it, and those who lose their life for my sake, and for the sake of the gospel, will save it" (Mark 8:35).

That mission, of giving life away for the sake of Jesus Christ, is the church's highest and holiest priority—to be the body of Christ in the world, a sign of God's reign.

The End? The Beginning?
Or the End of the Beginning?

*O*ne hundred years ago it was intellectually fashionable to predict the imminent demise of religion. Karl Marx had labeled religion the opiate of the masses and was confident that economic liberation in a classless state would, for the first time in history, render religion obsolete and irrelevant. Philosopher Friedrich Nietzsche declared that God was dead and that the church was God's mausoleum.

Not many would make those predictions at the beginning of the twenty-first century. In fact, something akin to the opposite of those dire predictions happened and continues to happen.

- Churches and religion not only did not disappear under Marx's political system, but became the inspiration and source of political rebellion that ultimately brought down the Communist governments of Eastern Europe.
- The church in China didn't die, but went underground only to emerge fifty years later, stronger, numerically larger, confident, and hopeful.
- Religion not only didn't disappear but emerged in the late twentieth and early twenty-first century in the arts, cinema, novels, and of all places, in the academic community, where a century ago, its demise was so confidently predicted.
- Scientists and theologians started talking to one another.
- Astronomers, astrophysicists, and cosmologists discovered that yesterday's certainty about the universe was superseded by the universe's expanding mystery, and in the process they started to sound like theologians.

- Health-care professionals wrote articles about the depth of the human spirit and the healing power of prayer.
- Courses on religion were presented to standing-room-only classes on American campuses. Theologian Harvey Cox's course on Christian ethics was among the most popular at Harvard.
- Christianity exploded in East Africa, and South American and "new" Christian churches in what were called third-world nations grew rapidly and began to look outward and to send missionaries, occasionally to the very nations of Europe and North America from which earlier missionaries had brought the gospel.
- Religion began to claim the attention of the secular media, and sales of books on religious topics skyrocketed.

Clearly something is happening, frequently outside the boundaries of the traditional churches. One conclusion is that the churches became outdated and irrelevant. But another, more biblical possibility is that God is up to something new in the world, as the prophet promised. Who is to say that the ferment, the renewed and sustained hunger for religion and religious meaning, is not the result of God's lively spirit moving in the world?

That's how it was in the beginning of our story, after all. The church was born in the heart of God at creation. The church is the historical extension of God's way of operating in and relating to the world—God's people, chosen, called, committed, and commissioned to live in the world as a sign of God's reign.

Modern historians are inclined to take a dim view of what became known as Constantinian Christianity. Historian Williston Walker called it "a fateful union with the state."[1] Some even argue that finally, after seventeen hundred years, Christendom, the Constantinian model of an officially approved, sanctioned, and sponsored church, has died, and the church is wondrously free to be faithful to Jesus Christ in new ways. Canadian theologian Douglas John Hall writes: "In Christian thinking endings can also be beginnings; and if we are courageous enough to enter into this ending thoughtfully and intentionally, we will discover a new beginning that may surprise us. The end of Christendom could be the beginning of something more nearly like the church—the disciple community described by the Scriptures."[2]

The church of Jesus Christ came into being as part of the Easter experience. After the crucifixion of Jesus, his followers did what any of us would do: hid, in fear and trembling, waiting for the furor to settle and for the opportunity to return to their jobs and families in Galilee—sad, but much wiser. Instead, the most incredible, most unexpected thing began to happen. The disciples continued to experience their friend Jesus as alive and present. The resurrection appearances related by the Gospel writers are in simple, straightforward language, almost as if the authors themselves can't believe they are actually writing them. Their friend and Lord was not dead. The worst the world could do to him had been proved ineffective. Jesus Christ was risen and present. Returning to their old lives was unthinkable in light of this new, Easter reality.

So they stayed together, the fledgling Easter community—the church. Slowly, cautiously, like a butterfly emerging from its chrysalis, they left their hiding place and began showing up in the Temple at prayers. And then, on the feast day of Pentecost, the church of Jesus Christ, the body of Christ in the world, was wondrously born.

Now the New Testament language becomes extravagant: "a sound like the rush of a violent wind . . . Divided tongues, as of fire . . . a tongue rested on each of them . . . All of them were filled with the Holy Spirit and began to speak in other languages, as the Spirit gave them ability" (Acts 2:2–4).

The immediate result, in addition to the marvelous new infusion of energy and power, was that communication began to happen. Pentecost pilgrims from other nations who were in Jerusalem for the festivities were witnesses to the phenomena, and most remarkable of all, "Each one heard them speaking in the native languages of each" (Acts 2:6).

The first characteristic of the church, after the energizing, empowering presence of the Holy Spirit, was—and is—communication. People speak and listen to each other. People talk and people hear. Dialogue, conversation, communication, and communion are given to the church by the Holy Spirit. And that ability, that divine gift, creates a community out of diverse nationalities. It was an amazing experience! "How is it that we hear?" they asked. "All were amazed. . . . Others sneered and said, 'They are filled with new wine'" (Acts 2:8, 12).

And then, out of this wonderful new community created by the Holy Spirit, one of them, Simon Peter, stood up and preached a sermon, proclaiming what God had done in Jesus Christ. In our beginning, the continuing presence of the risen Christ held his friends (the church) together; the Spirit gave them (the church) the energy and power needed and the ability to communicate, and the mission of the church was launched.

The presence of Christ—the gifts of the Spirit—the mission of the church—constitute the guiding sequence for the church's future in the twenty-first century.

And beneath it all, our worries, concerns, hopes, and aspirations, is the confidence that the church is God's idea, God's creation, God's precious partner. God builds the church in every age, and nothing, not even the power of hell itself, shall ever overcome it.

The Church of the Twenty-first Century

Some are already calling it the postdenominational age. We have already seen that one of the ways to characterize our era is "post-Constantinian." The old accommodation between church and empire/nation-state has finally come to an end. The last vestiges of the Protestant mainline churches' "establishment" in North American culture are disappearing. The "modern era," or modernity, the era of human history where most of the people living at the beginning of the twenty-first century came of age, was a time of unprecedented growth and progress. It seemed, after the horrors of World War II, the Holocaust, and the nuclear bombing of Hiroshima and Nagasaki, that the human race finally had learned the ultimate tragedy and futility of war. Technology and the expansion of economic and political freedom seemed finally capable of solving the historic scourges of hunger and disease. Modernity was the time when, in Dietrich Bonhoeffer's memorable phrase, humanity "came of age" and assumed responsibility for the life of the world. Rabbi Irving Greenberg characterizes modern civilization as humanity's attempt to "take charge of our own destiny," and when "the age-old Jewish and Christian promise of a world made whole for life seemed realizable by human efforts."[3]

If modernity was the time when human beings realized their own responsibility for what happens in their lives and societies, postmodernity is the time when not many of the old assumptions, the "givens," are valid any longer. The world, it turns out, is not as safe as we thought it had become. The violent attacks on the World Trade Center by religious ideological zealots was a sobering illustration of how our technological prowess and economic power could be turned against us. HIV-AIDS emerged as an out-of-control pandemic threatening a whole generation of Africans. Ethnic hatred emerged furiously in Central Europe and Asia, and the United States of America, the world's largest consumer of fossil fuels, refused to acknowledge its role in the planet-threatening reality of global warming.

In the postmodern world, everything had changed; nothing, it seemed, would ever be the same. The mainline church continued its numerical decline—which actually began in the middle of the last century—and its role in shaping, forming, and informing American culture continued to diminish. In fact, some are suggesting that the best, most creative thing the postmodern church could do would be to name and acknowledge its diminished status, which would mean ceasing frantic efforts to find someone to blame for the decline, and begin to ask and discern what God wants of the church in this new world.

Biblical scholar Walter Brueggemann says the church is now in something like "exile," a place different, indifferent, and sometimes hostile. But it is in no way a hopeless place. Brueggemann reminds us that God calls people in exile to important work. Rabbi Greenberg echoes the idea: "One of the most difficult trials facing Christianity is that having been a majority religion for most of its life, it is now entering into its own diaspora; the exile of Christianity in the secular world. Sometimes it distorts the personality as one seeks self-protection. . . . Sometimes the need for identity may lead to isolation or hostility or even hatred for the world." The Christian churches, Rabbi Greenberg wisely suggests, could learn something from the Jewish experience of being in exile.[4] Douglas John Hall goes even further and proposes that the end of Christendom, the final disappearance of the church's dominant, privileged, and powerful role in postmodern civilization, means an opportunity for the church to address and meet critical human needs. Hall says the end of Christendom could mean a new, healthy, life-giving, world-saving future for Christianity.

Historian Martin Marty, in a succinct study of the changing status of mainline churches, *Protestant Voices in American Pluralism*, traces this evolution: from 1607 Jamestown to 1955 (the publication date of Will Herberg's classic *Protestant, Catholic, and Jew*), from the dominant Colonial Big Three—Episcopalians, Presbyterians, Congregationalists—to the unprecedented religious diversity of contemporary American culture. There is no longer a dominant religious voice. Mainline Protestants constitute 25 percent of the American population; Evangelicals, Fundamentalists, and Pentecostals, 25 percent; African American Protestants, 8 percent.

Marty hopes we can avoid the "politics of nostalgia and resentment" as churches live into this new role in postmodern culture and avoid efforts to "retake America," which only reinforce our lost dominance. Instead, Professor Marty suggests that our hope lies in doing what we have done so faithfully in the past: building community, living a tradition, tending to spiritual and existential questions of meaning, and addressing whatever issues the world is struggling with, from our faith experience and tradition. Diversity, Marty says, is not going away. In fact, mainline Protestantism, with its "culture of flexibility and tolerance," helped bring it into being.

One thing seems certain. Denominational efforts to stop the loss of members in order to ensure institutional survival aren't very inspiring and don't work. Sitting in his Nazi prison cell as his church fought for its survival, Dietrich Bonhoeffer wrote haunting words:

> Our church, which has been fighting in these years only for its self-preservation, as though that were an end in itself, is incapable of taking the word of reconciliation and redemption to mankind and the world. . . . The Church is her true self only when she exists for humanity.[5]

The late Joseph Sittler, Lutheran theologian, wrote words in 1979 that resonate deeply at the beginning of the twenty-first century:

> The church in the next several decades is going to be a smaller, leaner, tougher company. I am convinced that the way for the church now is to accept the shrinkage, to penetrate the meaning and the threat of the prevailing secularity, and to tighten its mind around the task given to the critical cadre.[6]

But we have also seen that there is a strange resiliency within the church. Intentional persecution somehow is a source of spiritual renewal and courageous witness down through history. Even outright banishment only forces the church underground, where it learns to thrive and grow in new ways. Perhaps we should be careful about writing off the church as an obsolete anachronism whose time has come—and gone. And perhaps we should be cautious about dismissing denominations as worn-out vestiges of a bygone age. "Brand loyalty" is no longer strong or even existent for many. The old ethnic paradigm—Scots Presbyterians, German Lutherans—has broken down, and people choose churches on the basis of available parking, music, educational opportunities, and preaching. The ecumenical impulse within the gospel is drawing the old denominations closer together.

And yet, before dismissing the old denominations, perhaps the future will see a renewal of their institutional life, particularly as it expresses the gifts each one has received from the past and brings into the future: Lutheran-Anglican liturgy and sense of the church's apostolic history, for instance; or Presbyterian/Reformed commitment to the life of the mind, the intersection of theology and world, the right of conscience. Those denominational commitments are a precious legacy of the past, which will be even more relevant in the future ahead of us.

Epilogue

*T*here is work to be done by Christian people who love the church because it is God's precious creation and who want the church not merely to survive the threats of the postmodern, post-Christendom, postdenominational age, but actually to be the body of Christ; actually to convey the transcendence and mystery of God; actually to show the world what community looks like; actually to help men and women give their lives away, and in the process, save their lives. These people want the church to live that same secret of giving life away for the sake of the gospel, and in the process discovering and saving its own life.

They are people of all ages and all denominations who experience a lump in the throat and a tear in the eye when they stand within their own congregations and sing:

Though with a scornful wonder, this world sees her oppressed,
By schisms rent asunder, by heresies distressed,
Yet saints their watch are keeping; their cry goes up: "How long?"
And soon the night of weeping, shall be the morn of song.[1]

The saints are watching: our saints Peter and John, Augustine, Thomas Aquinas, Julian of Norwich, Teresa of Avila, Martin Luther, John Calvin; Presbyterians John Witherspoon, Marcus Whitman, Donaldina Cameron, Eugene Carson Blake, Lois Stair; ecumenical saints Dietrich Bonhoeffer, Martin Luther King Jr., Mother Teresa, Pope John XXIII, Bishop Tutu; and that particular community of saints who preceded each one of us and conveyed the gospel to us and showed each of us how to be followers of Jesus Christ and members of his body.

Each in their own way and their own time served Jesus Christ faithfully and courageously through the church. Each was impatient with the church. Each pushed the church to become more than it was. Each tired of the church's slowness. Each loved the church and its mission in the world.

Every church, every denomination, every congregation has its saints watching. And each has within it women, men, and children whom God will call and commission to be leaders and followers in the ongoing drama of God and God's creation, the story of the church.

Those men and women and children, each and every one of us, can be sure of the blessed challenge and promise:

> I am about to do a new thing;
> now it springs forth, do you not perceive it?
> (Isa. 43:19)

Notes

Prologue

1. Tertullian, *Apology,* AD 197.
2. Douglas John Hall, *The End of Christendom and the Future of Christianity* (Harrisburg, PA: Trinity Press International, 1995).
3. N. T. Wright, *Simply Christian: Why Christianity Makes Sense* (San Francisco: HarperSanFrancisco, 2006), x, xi.

Chapter 1. Looking Backward and Forward

1. Reynolds Price, *Letter to a Man in the Fire: Does God Exist and Does He Care?* (New York: Simon & Schuster, 1999).
2. *Time*, April 8, 1966.

Chapter 2. Behold, a Very Old Thing

1. Robert N. Bellah et al., *Habits of the Heart* (New York: Harper & Row, 1986), 221.
2. Wade Clark Roof, *A Generation of Seekers: The Spiritual Journeys of the Baby Boom Generation* (San Francisco: HarperSanFrancisco, 1993), 8.
3. James Weldon Johnson, "The Creation: A Negro Sermon," reprinted in *Black Voices: An Anthology of Afro-American Literature* (New York: Mentor, 1968), 364, from *God's Trombones* (1927).
4. The Fourth Lateran Council (1215) said, "There is but one universal Church of the faithful, outside which no one at all is saved" (Latin: "*Extra Ecclesiam nulla salus*").

Chapter 3. "I Believe in the Holy Catholic Church"

1. Annie Dillard, "The Gospel according to St. Luke," in *Incarnation: Contemporary Writers on the New Testament*, ed. Alfred Corn (New York: Viking, 1990), 36.

2. Robert Frost, "The Lesson for Today," in *Collected Poems, Prose, and Plays* (New York: Library of the Americas, 1995), 318.
3. "Blood of the martyrs," in *Apology*.

Chapter 4. Church, Empire, Reformation

1. Williston Walker, *A History of the Christian Church* (New York: Charles Scribner's Sons, 1959), 208–9.
2. John Emerich Edward Dalberg-Acton, letter to Bishop Mandell Creighton (April 5, 1887), in *The History of Freedom* (Grand Rapids: Acton Institute, 1993).
3. Roland H. Bainton, *Here I Stand: A Life of Martin Luther* (New York: Mentor, 1950), 59–60.
4. "'I cannot and I will not retract anything, since it is neither safe nor right to go against conscience.' Some reports have him adding, 'I cannot do otherwise, here I stand' and then, 'May God help me. Amen'" (Martin E. Marty, *Martin Luther* [New York: Lipper/Viking, 2004], 68).
5. John Calvin, *Institutes of the Christian Religion* 4.9.11; ed. John T. McNeill, trans. Ford Lewis Battles, LCC (Philadelphia: Westminster Press, 1960), 1174.
6. Dietrich Bonhoeffer, *Letters and Papers from Prison*, new greatly enlarged ed., ed. Eberhard Bethge and Collier Brooks (New York: Macmillan 1953, 1967, 1971), 369. The complete statement reads: "During the last year or so I've come to know and understand more and more the profound this-worldliness of Christianity. . . . I'm still discovering right up to the moment, that it is only by living completely in this world that one learns to have faith" (letter to Eberhard Bethge, July 21, 1944).

Chapter 5. Reformation to Revolution

1. Williston Walker, *A History of the Christian Church* (New York: Charles Scribner's Sons, 1959), 358.
2. James H. Smylie, *A Brief History of the Presbyterians* (Louisville, KY: Geneva Press, 1996), 30.
3. Ibid., 57.
4. Ibid.
5. Dean K. Thompson, "Celebrating Our Presbyterian Heritage: John Witherspoon, James Madison, and the U.S. Constitution," *Presbyterian Outlook*, July 4, 1991.
6. Ibid., 65.

Chapter 6. A New Church for a New World

1. Sydney E. Mead, *The Lively Experiment: The Shaping of Christianity in America* (New York: Harper & Row, 1963), 59.

Chapter 7. The Church as Living Reminder

1. Kathleen Norris, *Dakota: A Spiritual Geography* (New York: Houghton Mifflin, 1993), 161–62.
2. Walter Isaacson, "In Search of the Real Bill Gates," *Time*, June 24, 2001, www.time.com/time/printout/0,8816,137132,00.html (accessed November 1, 2007).

Chapter 8. The Church as Beloved Community

1. Martin E. Marty, "Religious Cause, Religious Cure," *The Christian Century*, February 28, 1979.
2. Jonathan Swift, *Thoughts on Various Subjects*, in *Miscellanies* (1711; London: Charles Bathurst, 1745).
3. See L. Gregory Jones, *Embracing Forgivness* (Grand Rapids: William B. Eerdmans Publishing Co., 1995), 12.
4. David Cairns, *Worship Now: A Collection of Services and Prayers for Public Worship* (Glasgow: St. Andrews Press, 1972), 56, citing William Barclay.
5. Anne Lamott, *Traveling Mercies: Some Thoughts on Faith* (New York: Pantheon Books, 1999), 54–55.

Chapter 9. A Sign of the Kingdom

1. *The Constitution of the Presbyterian Church (U.S.A.)*, Part II, *Book of Order* (Louisville, KY: Office of the General Assembly, 1999), G-1.0200.
2. Irving Greenberg, *For the Sake of Heaven and Earth: The New Encounter between Judaism and Christianity* (Philadelphia: Jewish Publication Society, 2004), 39, 44, 55.
3. Walter Brueggemann, *The Covenanted Self* (Minneapolis: Augsburg Fortress, 1999).
4. Told to the author by Steve Kurtz, Presbyterian Church (U.S.A.) mission worker, Osijek, Croatia, April 1997.

Chapter 10. The End? The Beginning?
Or the End of the Beginning?

1. Walker, *History of the Christian Church*, 102.
2. Douglas John Hall, *The End of Christendom and the Future of Christianity* (Harrisburg, PA: Trinity Press International, 1995), 51.
3. Greenberg, *For the Sake of Heaven and Earth*, 85.
4. Ibid., 116–17.
5. Bonhoeffer, *Letters and Papers from Prison,* 300, 239.
6. Joseph Sittler, *Grace Notes and Other Fragments* (Philadelphia: Fortress, 1981), 99.

Epilogue

1. Samuel John Stone, "The Church's One Foundation," in *The Pres-byterian Hymnal* (Louisville, KY: Westminster/John Knox Press, 1990), 442.